WORD PLAY

Fun Games for Building Reading and Writing Skills in Children with Learning Differences

LORI GOODMAN
& LORA MYERS

Contemporary Books

Chicago   New York   San Francisco   Lisbon   London   Madrid   Mexico City
Milan   New Delhi   San Juan   Seoul   Singapore   Sydney   Toronto

Library of Congress Cataloging-in-Publication Data

Goodman, Lori (Lori H.)
    Wordplay : fun games for building reading and writing skills in children
with learning differences / Lori Goodman and Lora Myers.
        p.   cm.
    Includes bibliographical references and index.
    ISBN 0-07-140821-5
       1. Reading games.   2. Reading—Parent participation.   I. Title:
Wordplay.   II. Myers, Lora.   III. Title.

    LB1525.55.G66   2003
    371.91'44—dc21   2003046148

1 2 3 4 5 6 7 8 9 0   AGM/AGM   2 1 0 9 8 7 6 5 4 3

ISBN 0-07-140821-5

Interior design by Susan H. Hartman
Illustrations by Paul Boyd

McGraw-Hill books are available at special quantity discounts to use as premiums and
sales promotions, or for use in corporate training programs. For more information,
please write to the Director of Special Sales, Professional Publishing, McGraw-Hill, Two
Penn Plaza, New York, NY 10121-2298. Or contact your local bookstore.

This book is printed on acid-free paper.

To my wonderful boys,
Isaac and Emmett. I love you more than chocolate!
—L.G.

To my first and best reading teachers,
Irene Myers and Shirley Perlman
—L.M.

AaBbCcDdEeFfGgHhIiJjKkLlMmNnOoPpQqRrSsTtUuVvWwXxYyZz

Contents

Preface

eading and writing first brought Lori Goodman and me together. For several years I had been teaching basic literacy classes for hospital workers in New York City and was beginning to understand the pervasiveness of learning disabilities among adults who struggle with print. With a fellow teacher, I got funding to set up a learning center where adults with special needs could get one-on-one instruction. Lori, a playwright and teacher whom I had recently met, volunteered as a tutor. We all created lively teaching materials, including a range of phonics games, that would help our learners strengthen their reading and writing skills. Three years later, when I was asked to create a citywide literacy program for #1199, the hospital workers' union, I left the learning center in Lori's capable hands.

Although our working lives took us in different directions, Lori and I kept up with each other. I celebrated the birth of her children, Isaac and Emmett, and introduced them to some of my favorite children's books (which they still enjoy). When Lori began to suspect that her older son, Isaac, was having trouble keeping up in school, I became a party to the struggle we describe in this book. I was impressed by Lori's persistence in dealing with New York City's maddeningly bureaucratic department of special education, and I was moved by her sensitivity to Isaac's emotional as well as academic needs.

One day Lori mentioned that she and her husband had invented some reading and writing games to play with Isaac at home. These games incorporated special techniques that we had used with adults in our learning center. It struck me that we should compile those games and develop new ones to help other parents whose children were struggling, like Isaac, but who didn't have our experience in teaching basic literacy.

The result is this book, which features step-by-step instructions for reading and writing games that help children learn. We've included basic information about reading instruction that will help parents and caregivers get the most out of the games. We hope this book will help you foster a relaxed and playful approach to learning for the whole family.

Acknowledgments

ur thanks to all the good people who offered their advice, encouragement, and critical reading skills as we wrote this book: Joan Behar, Paul Boyd, Amy Goodman, Claire Goodman, Andrew Kolker, Ida Kolker, and Lisa Remez.

Special thanks to Dr. Bonnie Goldblatt and Lainie Rosenblatt of the Churchill School in New York City, Linda Selvin of the New York branch of the International Dyslexia Association, and John M. Vinopal at renfaire.com.

And very special thanks to our little research assistants, who cheerfully field-tested the games with us: Isaac and Emmett Goodman-Boyd, Michael Goodman, Antonio Jubela-Gordon, Thea and Leanna Ross Marans, and Keithlyn Belle Parkman.

AaBbCcDdEeFfGgHhIiJjKkLlMmNnOoPpQqRrSsTtUuVvWwXxYyZz

Introduction

A Parent's Story

ive-year-old Isaac was happy in kindergarten at the local public school. He was eager to be there and enjoyed his classmates. Although my husband, Paul, and I noticed that he couldn't hold a crayon properly and alternated hands when he wrote his name, we weren't concerned. This was *kindergarten*, after all. We knew our son would develop at his own pace.

Even though Isaac had trouble writing, we were confident he would be a great reader. We had been reading to him constantly since he was an infant, and he really, *truly* loved books. So at our first parent-teacher conference we were stunned when Isaac's teacher told us he might not be academically ready for the rigors of first grade. Specifically, she felt that Isaac wasn't "reading ready." Reading ready? When we were his age, kindergarten meant playing the triangle and looking forward to snack time. Being "reading ready" was not expected of any five year old!

Nevertheless, for the rest of the year we made sure Isaac got whatever extra help was available at school. We read to him at home in a more focused way—pointing out words, reading slowly, and pausing more often to ask him what was happening and what might come next. And we enrolled him in the summer school reading program.

The extra schoolwork paid off: Isaac's first-grade year was uneventful, although, as a precaution, he continued to get extra help with reading. He was praised by the teacher for his devotion to books. After school he always did his reading homework first, and when questioned he showed that he understood the story. He moved easily on to second grade.

Then one day toward the end of his first semester, Isaac came home with something on his mind. "Mom," he said, "I have a secret. Everyone thinks I can read. But I can't."

I was so upset I wanted to cry. My sadness turned to guilt: what had I missed? And confusion: why hadn't the teacher noticed he had a problem?

We immediately asked the school to evaluate Isaac. The evaluation team confirmed that he was having reading difficulties. However, we were told his test scores did not show a big enough deficit to merit the support of special education services. The evaluators implied that he was lazy and had emotional problems that were getting in the way of his learning.

Paul and I were furious. We knew that Isaac was far from lazy, and he certainly—by all accounts, not just his parents'—had no emotional or behavioral issues that interfered with his desire to learn. This was a child who had proudly told us many times, "I was born to read!" We knew that our son, who had come to us in distress about his difficulties, had a real reading problem that the evaluators were dismissing.

Luckily, our principal had already created a program for at-risk children. He arranged for Isaac to work with a reading specialist two times a week. For the rest of the year we kept in constant touch with the specialist and the classroom teacher so that every evening we could reinforce at home what Isaac was doing at school.

At the beginning of third grade, we met with Isaac's new teacher. She immediately told us that Isaac was struggling greatly with reading. "I'm amazed that he's not crying every day," she said. "He's really bright, and this must be very frustrating for him. He's lucky he has great coping abilities!"

Paul and I immediately arranged for another evaluation by a private psychologist. She said the testers at school were wrong: Isaac wasn't lazy. She had observed that he was a very hard worker. But she had also observed that he hadn't acquired the basic skills he needed to become a competent reader. The psychologist gave Isaac's problem a name: *dyslexia*—a learning disability that is commonly characterized by a variety of difficulties with oral and written language.

Armed with the new evaluation, we went back to the school and arranged for Isaac to receive more special education services. Now he was pulled out of his regular class every day for intensive reading instruction. And we redoubled our efforts at home. Not a moment went by that we didn't turn into a reading lesson. We also joined the New York branch of the International Dyslexia Association, (IDA), an organization dedicated to helping dyslexic adults and children and their families.

A couple of months later, confusing information and advice started coming from every direction. The special education teacher said Isaac's reading problem wasn't as bad as his writing problem—his spelling and handwriting were way below grade level. His classroom teacher agreed, adding that math was also a big challenge. And since Isaac had a lot of trouble following instructions and getting started on his work in class, she strongly suspected he had an attention disorder. The private tutor we had hired strongly disagreed, although she said that Isaac had a lot of trouble focusing on skills that were hard for him. Our friends dismissed the "learning-disabled" label altogether, insisting that Isaac was bright and attentive. He just needed more time.

But deep down we knew that all of Isaac's difficulties in school stemmed from his not having yet acquired the building blocks of reading. There was no time to see if the skills would simply *kick in*: the system was marching along at its own relentless pace, raising the standards bar higher and higher but without providing adequate instruction for our son and children like him.

At this point Isaac was working overtime on reading, writing, and math. For the first time, he resisted going to school. And despite all his hard work, his teacher advised us to hold him back. Repeat third grade? A bad idea according to the IDA, which maintains that it doesn't do any good to hold back a child with average or above-average intelligence who has a learning disability. Simply repeating a grade and getting the same type of instruction would be like speaking louder to a person who doesn't speak English.

Instead the IDA recommends promoting the child—but using teaching methods that meet the child's special needs. The most effective method, known in the world of special education as the *multisensory approach*, combines seeing, hearing, and movement in the teaching of reading and writing. The theory goes that by developing strong links among seeing a word, saying a word, and writing a word, children with learning difficulties can successfully absorb the rules that most children seem to pick up so easily.

We knew Isaac would benefit from the multisensory approach—but his special education teacher wasn't able to use it consistently. She was working with a small group from Isaac's class, each with different needs, giving them extra help with schoolwork. Although she could occasionally slip in some multisensory instruction in basic reading, she could not give Isaac the intensive teaching he required. And because we had to focus on helping him keep up with his schoolwork, we were in the same situation. In effect, Isaac was getting a triple dose of the same class work but little instruction to address his underlying problems with reading.

No wonder he was starting to melt down. Our happy, playful family life was turning into boot camp. Weekends too often became extensions of bad school weeks, with reviews and drills replacing drawing, playground hopping, and storytelling. There was no time just to have fun.

Not surprisingly, my husband and I were stressed as well. We were tired of looking at our son as a walking bundle of deficits—the way the school defined him. We were tired of dwelling on his weaknesses instead of celebrating his strengths. To us, Isaac wasn't disabled—he simply needed a different approach to reading and lots more practice than some of his classmates to master the basics.

We decided to experiment with different learning strategies at home. But we wanted them to be fun. We knew there had to be a way to teach Isaac without turning our home into another schoolroom. There had to be a way to create a safe harbor from the storm of skill and drill. And then it hit me.

We had always been great believers in the idea that for children playing is learning. Put another way, playing is children's "work." Although child psychologists stress the importance of play for the very young, a lot of parents understand that even as kids get older, play is still an effective way to learn.

We had been making up games and stories since Isaac was a baby. He loved them. Surely we could find games that would help him improve his basic reading skills. The ideal game would combine academic and physical stimulation—a homegrown version of the multisensory approach recommended by the IDA. And because of Isaac's active imagination—one of his greatest strengths—we knew that he would be happy to invent some games himself. We reasoned that through games we could restore the playful feeling that had been missing from our family life. Plus, by now his little brother, Emmett, was old enough to play along.

The first opportunity came during the winter break. We were in New England for a weekend of cross-country skiing. The minute we checked into the hotel and the boys saw two double beds, the game—spontaneously—began. As I watched them jumping from bed to bed, I grabbed my backpack and pulled out paper and markers. While Paul was unloading the car, I put a few "problem" letters on pieces of paper. Then I asked Isaac, as he leapt, to look at the letter I was holding up and to SHOUT its sound as loud as he could. Giving him permission to whoop it up did the trick: he was too excited to resist the "lesson." As the game progressed, he began—on his own—thinking of words that began with the sounds he was shouting out. It didn't take long before Emmett joined in, repeating his brother's "phonics" cries.

Letter/Sound/Word Jump sparked a marathon of games. In the restaurant we played a phonics version of I Spy ("I spy with my little eye something that begins with the sound mmmmm"—menus? milk shake? mushy vegetables?). Out on the ski trail we played a vocabulary game, Can You Top This? (My toes are freezing, icicles, frostbitten—mummified!) And each night at bedtime we would read a chapter from a book and make predictions about what would happen next.

Back home, we kept discovering new games or making up our own. We tried out Vowel Stories—drawing on Isaac's strengths as a storyteller to reinforce his recognition of vowel sounds and to build his vocabulary. We devised Words All Over Me—taping words onto parts of our bodies that followed similar spelling patterns: like *farm, harm, charm* on the arm and *rack, stack, pack* on the back. Over the next semester we played a game a week to strengthen our son's reading skills. Gradually he regained his excitement about going to school.

The payoff came at the spring parent-teacher conference: Isaac's teacher told us that he had greatly improved in his reading and in his overall performance in class. We know the games contributed to his success.

Isaac continues to have difficulty with reading and writing even now that he attends a special school for children who learn differently. But these games still help him over the rough spots. And the bonus is Isaac enjoys playing them with his brother, Emmett, who, as it turns out, also has learning difficulties.

Playing these games has also helped Paul and me release a lot of the anxiety we felt watching our children suffer in school. We are confident that when all is said and done—and read—we did everything we could to ensure that Isaac and Emmett will remember their childhood as a time of joy, not of humiliation.

If this story sounds familiar, we hope the games we've compiled in this book will motivate you to take an active role in your child's development as a competent reader and writer.

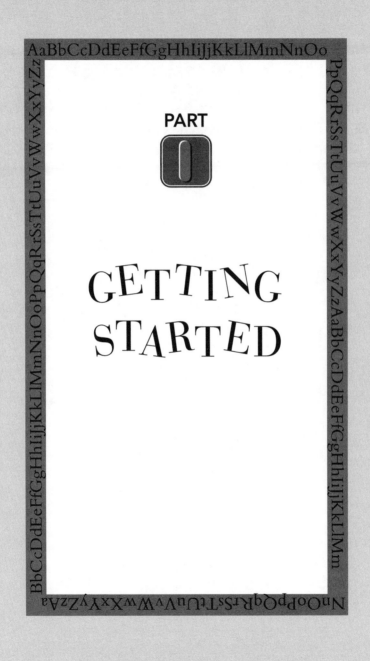

PART

0

GETTING
STARTED

AaBbCcDdEeFfGgHhIiJjKkLlMmNnOoPpQqRrSsTtUuVvWwXxYyZz

Before You Play

ou can find a million different books on how to teach children who have trouble with reading and writing. Most of them look like college texts. You become overwhelmed before you finish the first page. Other books require extensive materials and preparation that no adult in an active family has time to assemble.

This is not one of those books. This is a book of games, most of which help children practice and master different aspects of reading and writing. There are also games that prompt children to organize their thoughts, to strengthen their memory, and to improve their spoken language and motor skills.

Before you play these games with your child, you need to understand that reading is a complex process that involves many skills working simultaneously. Most books will tell you that kids who have trouble with reading are struggling with one or more of the following areas:

- **Phonics**—understanding and remembering that each letter represents a specific sound. When you read certain combinations of letters, you must translate them into a spoken word (reading teachers call this *decoding*).
- **Vocabulary**—understanding and remembering the meaning of words and how they are changed by prefixes and suffixes and the sentences they're in.
- **Comprehension**—fully understanding and remembering the meaning of a story, poem, or other written material; understanding how to use clues in the story ("context clues") to figure out unfamiliar words.

In practice, all these aspects of reading are intertwined. Decoding may be the initial stumbling block for your child, and yet his comprehension may be excellent. On the other hand, just because he can decode doesn't mean he automatically understands what he's reading. As a child gets older and faces more challenging material and vocabulary, comprehension and the ability to acquire new words from the story may weaken.

A child may also have problems paying attention, recalling what she has read, or catching herself when she's misread a word. So when you are told that your child has trouble with reading, even an expert may not know exactly what's going wrong. There may be multiple reasons for her difficulty, each affecting and compounding the other.

What, then, can a parent do to help? More than likely, your child is weary of being taught formally. So much of the school day is already devoted to intensive reading and writing (sometimes starting in preschool these days!), not to mention extra services: tutoring, special education classes, summer school, and—in some cases—speech and language therapy and occupational therapy. Your child may be anxious about seeing his peers forge easily ahead while he lags behind. And when you get involved, as all responsible parents do, he may mistake your concern as disappointment or as a sign you think he's stupid.

You'll probably agree that the things children do willingly and enthusiastically are the things they find fun or appealing. That's the premise behind using games to practice those aspects of reading that give your child the most trouble. More important, you want to provide an experience different from the one she's having in the classroom. You want to turn your home into a place where she feels safe, smart, confident, in control, open to learning and exploration, and willing to take risks. Above all, you want your child to feel that you're on her side.

This sounds like a tall order—but it's not. You first need to ask yourself some basic questions and do a little homework. Here are some ideas for getting started.

Talk to Your Child's Teachers

It's important for you to get a clear idea of the reading problems your child is wrestling with. Ask the teacher to specify the areas of weakness and to tell you what's being done to address them. If you know the classroom teacher or special education teacher is working on phonics, you might reinforce letter-sound connections with a game at home. The more specific information you get—the sounds, the letters, the word patterns—about what your child is working on in school, the more useful the game will be. If you can't get this information from the teacher, for whatever reason, observe your child as he's doing homework and note where he's getting stuck.

However, you don't have to replicate what's going on in school. The main idea is to get the teacher to help you identify the underlying weaknesses or gaps in your child's reading strategies, regardless of what the class is studying at the moment. Then you can pick games that help close those gaps. Or you might want to use games for review, to make sure old lessons have been mastered: many children with learning differences need constant repetition and review that teachers, under pressure to move forward, can't always provide.

Talk Honestly with Your Child About the Problem

How aware is your child that she has a reading difficulty? Can she explain what part of reading is hardest—and what part comes easily? Are her difficulties a source of distress? How can you allay her feelings of frustration/stupidity? It's important for your child to recognize she has a problem without becoming overwhelmed or demoralized by it.

You need to find gentle ways to discuss her problems and her feelings about them. It's up to you to help your child put everything in perspective and make her understand you're a full partner in learning. Talk about the future—how your child's strengths will play out later on in life. Let her know she can learn things that don't come easily. Point out examples—and remind her of the aids grown-ups use: calculators, spell checks . . . secretaries!

Observe Your Child

Of course you already do. But now focus your attention. What are your son's or daughter's specific strengths and passions? (For instance, is he a natural storyteller, or is she crazy about trucks?) Is there a way to use these strengths and passions to solve reading problems? For example, Isaac's great sense of humor prompts something silly to happen in every game. He also loves superheroes, like Batman, so he involves action figures in many games. If your child loves physical activity, you can use that energy to advantage.

If you have difficulty finding a clear-cut strength or interest, don't worry. Observe what your child does when he plays independently in his free time. Keep trying new things and approaches until you stumble on the right idea. And you will. That's an education in itself.

Take Stock of Your Strengths and Weaknesses

You're in on this too. Do you like to draw, make up stories, or be physically active? Think about the things you enjoy doing with your child. If *you're* having fun, reading practice won't feel like a chore. However, if you're bored and short on patience, your child may pick up on your irritation and possibly blame himself for that.

Identify a Small Number of Areas to Work on at One Time

Most of the Wordplay games exercise specific aspects of reading. Get your child actively involved in choosing the skills to practice. After every game, reward him with praise—the best kind is realistic and concrete. Don't just say "Good job!" Rather, point out a specific accomplishment, such as reading a difficult vowel sound correctly. Also praise him for perseverance and patience.

Don't shy away from the occasional bribe. Some children need instant—and tangible—gratification. You can keep a chart that details the specific skills your son or daughter needs to practice. Every time you play a game that addresses that skill, put a check on the chart next to it. (In Isaac's case, after ten check marks, he gets to buy a small toy or to decide on a family activity or outing. More and more he forgets about the rewards and is happy just to award himself a big fat check for a job well done.)

Involve Siblings if You Can

A younger child can benefit from the games you play, and an older child can help teach a little sister or brother. One of the unexpected benefits for Isaac is that now he enjoys teaching his younger brother, Emmett, a skill he has mastered.

Learn as You Play

You don't have to be a reading expert to play Wordplay games. You'll develop your own expertise the more you play and experiment with them. Use the Appendix (where noted in the games) to guide you. Don't be afraid to make mistakes; just try again. That's how we learn. By tackling a problem together, and showing that you're not afraid to fail, you are helping your child develop strategies that will be useful long after reading ceases to be a challenge.

How to Play Wordplay Games

 t bears repeating: reading is a complex process that involves many skills working simultaneously. To improve, struggling young readers may have to tackle certain skills in isolation and practice them repeatedly. The games in this book have been organized according to a specific skill or combination of skills that a child, whatever his or her grade level, may need to strengthen. Many games have multiple benefits that focus on more than one skill at a time. Check the goals section of each game and the skills tables at the end of Chapter 3 to see which skills are targeted.

Where appropriate, Wordplay games refer you to one or more sections of the Appendix, where you will find important information about the basics of reading and writing and word lists to help you get started. The Appendix makes *Wordplay* a one-stop resource that spares you from having to search through volumes of reference materials in order to play a game effectively.

For example, the game Letter/Sound/Word Jump instructs you to choose a consonant and to check the Appendix before you play. If you've forgotten what a consonant is, or how many the alphabet contains, "The Alphabet" and the "Simple Basic Phonics" sections in the Appendix will refresh your memory. Or games that focus on letter combinations, word families, or parts of speech will direct you to the Appendix section for explanations and examples. After a while you will start to feel more confident about your knowledge of the basics.

The Basics of Reading

If reading always came easily to you, you probably don't remember much about how you learned. Here's a quick refresher course in the ABCs of the ABCs.

Phonics

Good readers have mastered the twenty-six letters of the alphabet and the sounds they make, singly and in combination. For children who have difficulty with print, learning how to break the "phonics code" is usually the hardest part of reading and writing. Unfortunately, straightforward phonics drills are often tedious and abstract. It is far, far better for a parent to work on decoding through games. The Wordplay phonics games present the building blocks of reading in different ways so that your child can keep practicing the same basic skills without getting bored.

Before you play a phonics game, check the "Simple Basic Phonics" section in the Appendix to learn about vowels, consonants, and letter combinations and select a few to focus on. Please note that in the instructions and appendices you may see a letter between slashes, like this /d/. This is the phonics notation indicating that you should say the sound the letter makes, in this case *duh* as in dog instead of the letter *d* as in *a, b, c, d.*

Sight Words and Word Families

There are hundreds of words in English called *sight words*, like *the, of,* and *to,* that either cannot be sounded out or occur so frequently it's best to memorize them so they can be read without hesitation or error. Some sight words—like *would, could,* and *should*—belong to the same word family; that is, they have several letters in common that can make memorizing and recognition easier. Again, because repetition is the key to learning sight words, a game that adds the element of fun to the repetitions—like "fishing" for words or throwing balls at words—helps your child stick with the task. Before you play a game involving sight words and word families, see the "Sight Words" section in the Appendix for sample lists.

Vocabulary

Children without an extensive vocabulary have a hard time understanding what they're reading, especially as they get older and reading material becomes more difficult. To complicate matters, most young readers, including different learners, have a larger spoken vocabulary than a reading vocabulary. Some children with reading problems may also have speech and language difficulties that interfere with their ability to find the right word to say in certain situations or to recall words they've learned recently. Wordplay vocabulary games help children expand their spoken vocabularies and/or match their reading vocabulary to their verbal abilities. We encourage the use of a children's dictionary when you play vocabulary games (see Recommended Reading).

Comprehension

The best way to make sure a child understands and remembers a story is to ask questions about words, sentences, or passages as you're reading along and/or to ask him to explain what's going on in the story every now and then. However, games can also reinforce discrete comprehension skills; for example, keeping ideas or events in the right order or sequence, recognizing the difference between a main idea and supporting details, retelling what happened in a story in one's own words, and becoming familiar with the variety of styles to be found in print, from advertisements to poetry. Children who have trouble following the story line in even the shortest book can particularly benefit from playing Wordplay games that focus on comprehension skills.

Writing

Writing and reading go together like macaroni and cheese. One skill relies on and nurtures development of the other—which is why it is not surprising that kids who struggle with reading usually struggle as well with the mechanics of writing—even those with lively imaginations! Because writing can seem daunting to a child who learns differently, many Wordplay games break down the process into manageable parts that children can handle. Some games prompt children to write single letters of the alphabet or short lists of simple words. Others encourage them to cut out printed words and sentences to build a new story. Prewriting games (games that spark thinking about things to write about) motivate children to tell stories through which they can develop a sense of a beginning, a middle, and an end and to distinguish main ideas from supporting details. These concepts are fundamental not only to writing stories but to reading and understanding stories as well.

Miscellaneous

Many other skills come into play when children read and write. We've targeted a choice group of them in our grab bag of miscellaneous games, such as breaking words up into syllables or units of sound, expressing one's thoughts clearly to others (developing expressive language), putting words into categories, learning correct spelling, and being able to recall a story or an instruction easily and accurately. Since many children with reading problems often have difficulty with physical coordination—what educators call *fine* and *gross motor* areas—we also include games that help kids improve their eye-hand coordination, left-right orientation, and handwriting.

Getting Started

When should you use which game and for what reason? The answer depends on your young reader's particular needs. As we've advised, the first step is to speak with your child's teachers to get a clear idea of specific areas of reading and writing difficulty. Next, turn to the game tables starting on page 24. Pick a game that targets one of those areas and that looks like an activity your child would enjoy. (Wordplay games can easily be played by you and one child unless indicated otherwise.)

As a rule of thumb, games that focus on phonics or the alphabet are probably the logical place to begin if you have a kindergartner or an older child with very low reading skills. Wordplay phonics games are easy to play and very active. If your child needs to repeat the same sounds over and over, she will more likely enjoy doing this in the context of a lively game rather than being asked to read sounds from flash cards.

Selecting Games to Play

There is no specific order to the games. Feel free to pick and choose one according to your child's needs and desires. Play the same game back-to-back or mix games up: alternate indoor games with outdoor ones, phonics workouts with vocabulary games, writing games with choices from the miscellaneous grab bag. Play a game a day or play several games in a row if you and your child have the energy!

In other words, use this book like a cookbook. Browse through it and try out one or two "recipes" at a time. Keep track of your child's favorites, return to them often, but try out new recipes every now and then.

Alternating Hard and Easy Games

You will quickly learn which games are too difficult for your child. This is important information that tells you what specific aspects of reading pose the greatest challenges. For example, did he have problems recognizing a certain letter or making its sound? Did he find writing a chore? Did he confuse one sight word with another? Or is he just not ready to tackle a particular skill? Keep notes about what caused problems in a small notebook. You can return to these games later, find another game that tackles the skill in a different way, or with your child's help, adapt the game to make it more manageable.

You can also use your own knowledge of your child's strengths to alter the game. For example, if your son has a strong visual sense, he may need more visual clues than the instructions provide. If your daughter likes to run around a lot, you may want to transfer an indoor game to a playground. It never hurts to modify a game—as long as you keep the focus on the reading skills.

On the other hand, don't abandon games that appear too easy for your child. Remember that most children who learn differently require greater amounts of repetition, review, and reinforcement than their teachers can provide in the classroom. Plus, it's always a good idea to make a child feel successful. So if you've played a game that your child found very challenging, follow it up with one you know your child can breeze through.

Remember . . .

Wordplay games are supplements for school, *not* substitutes for school-based learning and any special tutoring your child receives. Also, don't forget to read to and with all your children as much as you can. Make sure they see you reading on your own for enjoyment and information. Encourage your kids to read to you. Ask them to help you write shopping lists, cards, letters, and E-mails to friends and family. Invite them to write their own stories and poems.

Above all, keep in mind that Wordplay games are designed to be fun for the whole family. So keep them light—and let the games begin!

Behind the Games

The Multisensory Approach to Reading

ver wonder why it's so hard to memorize a poem from a book but a cinch to recall lyrics to a song you learned when you were young? Many experts in the field of special education would say we remember the song because we learned it by hearing the words combined with music and movement (dancing around our living room)—and, of course, by happily rehearsing the lyrics until we had mastered them. In other words, educators would tell us, we learned in a *multisensory* way that we found enjoyable enough to repeat.

The concept of multisensory learning is at the heart of most of the games in this book. It's an educational strategy that is supported by a growing body of research (see Recommended Reading). It is promoted by the International Dyslexia Association, which has pioneered the use of structured multisensory curricula with children who are identified as being dyslexic. This approach is used in many special education classrooms across the country and in some mainstream classes as well.

Simply put, a multisensory approach engages almost all the child's senses—sight, sound, touch, and movement (sometimes even taste!)—in the learning process. It is also based on the idea that children who learn differently are in need of more "direct instruction" than children who learn to read easily. That means struggling readers need to be taught basic concepts of reading—from phonics to comprehension—in step-by-step fashion, with ample time to review and repeat.

By multisensory we don't mean that all games involve dancing, jumping around, or other physical activity. Sometimes just reading, saying, and writing a word simultaneously provide enough of a workout for a special learner. But often children need to involve the larger muscles of their arms and legs to help them catch on to a particularly difficult reading or writing concept.

Many educators believe that our nation's fundamental approach to teaching is undergoing profound change. As we learn more about how the brain works, we are discovering that children come to school with many different styles of learning, which teachers need to identify and address. Some believe that the future holds customized education tailored to the specific learning style of each child.

Who knows if this new vision of education will materialize? But even if it does, *now* is when your child is struggling with schoolwork—and facing higher standards of learning measured by uniform yearly tests. Many public school teachers have not been trained in multisensory instructional techniques, and even those who know them are pressured increasingly to cover more and more material during the year, leaving them less time to devote to individual students who can't keep pace with the rest of the class. If your child is in this group, you *must* get involved. Games you play together that draw on multisensory techniques to teach reading and writing can enhance whatever instructional methods are being used in the classroom.

Materials

You don't need a closetful of materials to get started. You probably have most of them at home. Those that you do need to purchase will be a good investment—you'll use them again and again. And you might want to have a roomy tote bag handy to store them in.

- **Alphabet cards**—A set of alphabet cards is one of the best investments. You will find simple alphabet flash cards at most book and toy stores—or on the Internet. Or you can make your own using index cards or scraps of paper. Educational supply stores carry more advanced phonics packs that include different vowel and consonant combinations.

- **Three-dimensional letters and letter games**—You can find 3-D letters in book and toy stores. The idea is to have a tactile alphabet—on cubes or tiles or other materials—that a child can pick up and move around. More economically, you can cut out letters in felt or rough, colored cardboard or sandpaper. You should also have popular letter games such as Scrabble and Boggle.

- **Writing implements**—It should go without saying, but we'll say it anyway: always keep a good supply of paper, index cards, Post-its, pens, pencils (regular and multicolored), crayons, markers, and other writing tools on hand. (Recycling flyers and even old mail is a good idea—use the blank sides to jot things down!)

- **White/blackboard**—A small whiteboard (with erasable markers) or a blackboard (with chalk) is always useful. You can also use a Magna Doodle—an erasable writing surface for children.

- **Reference books**—A children's dictionary, a thesaurus, an encyclopedia, an atlas, an almanac—all of the above will come in handy. (See Recommended Reading for some of our favorites.)

- **Refrigerator magnets**—You probably have plenty of these already—to attach photographs or your child's drawings to the fridge. Think about using them to post a letter or a word you're concentrating on during game time. There are also some great prepackaged sets of magnetized letters or words for sale that are intended to be stuck on refrigerators and used to make sentences, poems, or short stories.

- **Old reading material**—Keep stacks of old newspapers, books, comics, magazines, take-out menus, flyers, and other reading materials to use for games.

- **Rewards and bribes**—Edible treats, toys, trading cards, or, even better, books, comic or otherwise: these are some of the rewards you want to have on hand for a job well done. Though praise may be enough, sometimes your child will need that extra bit of motivation to keep working at something difficult.

Games at a Glance

The following tables will help you quickly find games that target the specific skills you want to focus on with your child.

Table 1 lists all games chapter by chapter, with corresponding page numbers for easy reference.

Table 2 indicates all the skills that each game targets. Many games work on more than one skill simultaneously. For example, comprehension games also have a writing component; often a sight word game can help you build a child's vocabulary at the same time.

Table 1

Table 2

Games	Phonics	Sight Words	Vocabulary	Comprehension	Writing	Misc.
Letter/Sound/Word Jump	■					
Guess the Letter	■					
Touchy-Feely Alphabet	■					
Phonics in Action	■				■	Coordination
Squeaky-Clean Phonics	■				■	Motor skills
Words All Over Me	■		■		■	
Alpha Angels	■					
Finger Phonics	■					
I Spy Sounds	■					
Boggling Boggle	■		■			
Confusing Hopscotch	■					Motor skills
Crazy Ates		■	■			Rhyming
Set Your Sights		■	■			Coordination
Can You Top This?			■			
How Much Is That Word?			■			Addition
Room Sleuth			■		■	Categorizing
Odd or Peculiar?			■			Categorizing, Spelling
Red Light/Green Light		■				Motor skills
Packing for Adventure			■			Critical thinking
The Art in the Article			■			Skimming written material
Fishing for Words		■	■			Coordination
Dictionary Snack			■			Alphabetizing
Sight Word Suicide		■				Coordination

Games	Phonics	Sight Words	Vocabulary	Comprehension	Writing	Misc.
Fore and Aft			■	■		
Instant Replay				■		
What Do You Know?				■		Categorizing
Writing, Writing Everywhere				■		Categorizing
Lunchbox Surprise			■	■		
Exploding Story				■		
Breaking News				■	■	
Sequence Scramble				■		
Which Way to Go?			■	■	■	
Elizabethan Insults			■	■		
Hopping Sentences					■	Parts of speech
Label the House			■		■	
Unfolding Poetry					■	
Squeaky-Clean Tales					■	
Recycled Stories					■	
The Charlotte Game		■	■		■	
Vowel Stories	■				■	Expressive language
Caption It				■	■	
Word by Word					■	
Writing for Ransom		■	■	■	■	
Total Recall				■		Following multi-step instructions
What If						Problem solving
Category Pitch			■			Classifying

Table 2 continues on page 28

Games	Phonics	Sight Words	Vocabulary	Comprehension	Writing	Misc.
Dom-in-o, Dom-in-oes	■		■			Syllabication
Memory Café					■	Memory building, note taking
Keyboard Kinetics	■	■	■		■	Computer skills
From Here to There	■	■	■		■	Spelling
Bang the Word Slowly	■		■			Syllabication
Pillow Jumps						Coordination, memory building
War						Expressive language, motor skills
Sleight of Mind			■			Memory building

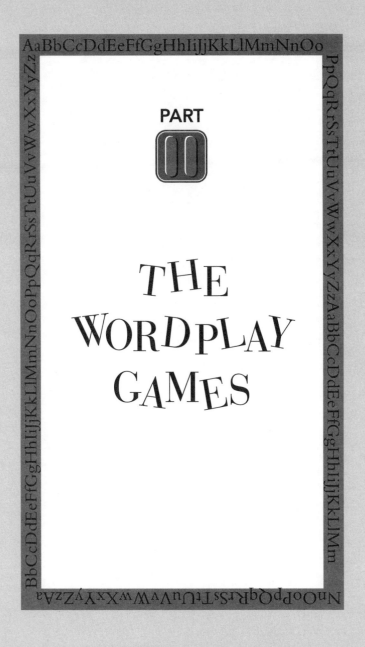

PART

II

THE
WORDPLAY
GAMES

ABC Phonics Games

ithout knowing the letters of the alphabet and the sounds they make, you wouldn't be able to read this book. So we shouldn't have to convince you that automatic recognition of letters and sounds is the foundation of fluent and pleasurable reading.

The games in this section will help your child achieve that automatic recognition. As you play, remember to keep it simple. Make sure your child has mastered single sounds before moving on to more complex combinations of letters.

Always Remember

- If you see that your child isn't enjoying the game, stop playing. Ask why she didn't like it. Get her ideas about how to make it better.

- At the end of every game, take stock together of the skills you worked on. Be lavish with praise for the things your child did well and be encouraging about the things she found difficult. Be as specific as possible.
- If your child is upset about something that's hard for her to do, remind her of the things she does well. Assure her of your faith in her ability to learn.

Letter/Sound/Word Jump

See it, say it, jump it!

Goals: Quickly recognize a letter and its sound.
Materials: Paper, markers or crayons.
When/Where: This game requires space for a child to jump and license to shout at the top of her lungs. You can play this on a bed, on a trampoline, or at a pool.
The Game: On separate pieces of paper, write five letters that your child is having trouble with and two or three letters that your child already knows. Review the name of each letter and the sound it makes. Start with consonants, since they're easier to learn, and then move to vowels. (See "The Alphabet" and "Simple Basic Phonics" in the Appendix.)

After the review, tell your child to start jumping and shouting. Then tell her you're going to hold up one letter at a time. (1) As soon as she sees it, she must shout the name of the letter and the sound it makes. (2) If she does this correctly, put a check on the paper. (3) If she earns three checks, she gets to grab the paper and keep it. (4) If your child has trouble doing this, you call out the letter and sound and have her repeat it.

Variations

■ Once the child has mastered the letter and the sound, the next time you play, go directly to the word: See the letter and yell out a word that begins with the letter.

■ When your child has mastered the individual letters/sounds, move to consonant blends and words that begin with blends. (See "Consonant Blends" in the Appendix.)

■ For more of a challenge, use ending sounds. For example, /p/ in *hop* or /mp/ in *jump.*

Tips

■ Show the letters in a different order every time.

■ Write all consonants in one color and all vowels in another color.

■ Every time you play this game, make sure you include letters you think your child knows. It never hurts to review.

■ If you don't have anything safe for your child to jump on, adapt the game. For example, have your child run in a circle and grab the piece of paper—like a brass ring—and shout out the letter/sound.

■ Be alert to what your child finds difficult—and what she finds easy.

■ Before each round of the game, ask your child to help you pick letters she'd like to practice.

Touchy-Feely Alphabet

Get letters off the page—and into your child's hands!

Goals: Reinforce the connection between letters and sounds.

Materials: A set of 3-D alphabet letters in wood or plastic. Or, if you have time to make your own 3-D alphabet, buy a few sheets of sandpaper, felt, or any material with a distinct tactile quality. Cardboard is fine if there's nothing else available—but be sure to decorate the letters with something scratchy or bumpy, such as sparkles or sand. With your child, trace twenty-six block-format letters onto the material you've chosen and cut them out. Make each letter at least two inches high—or big enough to handle comfortably.

When/Where: Anywhere, anytime—as long as you have your set of Touchy-Feely letters with you.

The Game: Put all the Touchy-Feely letters in a big box or paper bag. Begin only with a few letters if your child is really struggling with the alphabet. (See "The Alphabet" in the Appendix.) Then, with eyes closed or blindfolded, the first player reaches into the container and pulls out a letter. The goal is to identify the letter by its shape and make its sound—no peeking! For extra points, the player can say a word that begins with that letter. Vowels can either be long or short (see "Simple Basic Phonics" in the Appendix); that is, your child can say /ā/ as in *acorn* or /ă/ as in *apple*. *Y* should be read as a consonant, as in *young*, to start, before you move on to read it as a vowel, as in *my* or *baby*.

Repeat, taking turns, until the entire alphabet has been felt, touched, and spoken for!

Variations

- When you see that your child has mastered each letter and its sound, go directly to whole words: feel the letter and say a word.

- To make the game more complicated, ask each player to identify the letter's category: vowel or consonant.

- If your child has more trouble with vowels than with consonants, pull out the consonants and play only with *a, e, i, o, u*, and *y*. Or vice versa: eliminate the vowels.

- At more advanced stages, pull out three or four letters and "feel" whether they make a word. If not, go back to the container and feel for a letter that will complete the word.

Tips

- If you're making your own letters, use a stencil if you don't have a steady hand.

- If your child is struggling to name a letter or think of a word, help her along. Say it for her and have her repeat it.

Phonics in Action

Alphabet charades make letters come alive.

Goals: Reinforce letter sounds and practice writing.
Materials: A hat or sock filled with letters (Scrabble tiles, letter magnets, etc.), paper, and a pen.

When/Where: Anywhere there is space to move around. Best when you have more than two players.

The Game: Put all the letters in the hat. Player number one picks a letter and puts it on the table or the floor for all to see. The player must think of a word that begins with that letter and write it on a piece of paper, which he turns face down. Then he acts it out until one of the other players guesses the word. The player shows everybody the word he has written. The person who guessed the word takes the next turn.

If your child has great difficulty recognizing letters, an adult player should say the letter and its sound and secretly help the child pick a word to act out.

Variations

- Increase the difficulty of the game: don't show the letter. Players must guess the word and the letter it starts with.
- If your child resists writing, he can pull out a letter and act out the word that begins with the letter without writing it. You can write the letter and word after his turn.

Tips

- If your child has difficulty writing, you can write the word, and he can copy it after his turn is over.
- If your child can write, don't make an issue of spelling, but don't let misspellings go uncorrected. Look up the words in a dictionary once the game is finished.

Squeaky-Clean Phonics

Vandalize the bathroom wall and come out smarter and cleaner.

Goals: Reinforce the connection between letters and sounds.

When/Where: The bathtub.

Materials: Foam soap, bath paints or crayons, or shaving cream; a tiled bathroom wall or a mirror; a water squirt bottle or sponge; paper or index cards; pencils or markers.

The Game: Before bath time, write a few letters that your child is having trouble with on separate pieces of paper or index cards. Then, while she's soaking in the tub, review the names of the letters and the sounds they make. Start with consonants since they are easier to remember than vowels. (See "The Alphabet" and "Simple Basic Phonics" in the Appendix.)

Next, give your child the can of foam soap. When she's ready, say the sound of one of the letters and tell her to write the corresponding letter as large as she can on the tiled wall. Or hold up a card with a letter on it and have her say the name of the letter and the sound it makes as she spray-writes it.

If she writes the correct letter in response, give her the squirt bottle or sponge to clean the letter off the wall (using the squirt bottle helps your child strengthen hand muscles at the same time). Then move on to another sound/letter.

If she writes the wrong letter or she writes the right letter incorrectly, clean the wall and, with the can of soap, spray the letter on the palm of her hand. Ask your child to respray the letter correctly on the wall.

Variations

- Spread the foamy shaving cream or soap all over the wall at the start. Have your child use her finger to make the letters. You can also use bath crayons or bath paints.
- When your child has mastered individual letters/ sounds, move to blends and words that begin with blends. (See "Consonant Blends" in the Appendix.)
- Substitute sight words, like *the, and, with* (see "Sight Words" in the Appendix), or words your child has trouble spelling.
- If you prefer—or if your family takes showers instead of baths—use a steamy mirror and finger-write the letters.

Tips

- Every time you play this game, include letters your child knows. It never hurts to review.
- Make sure you end on a letter your child knows so that she finishes the game with a success.
- Some bath foams come in different colors. Use different colors for vowels and consonants.

Guess the Letter

A game that Isaac made up to help his little brother, Emmett.

Goals: Learn the alphabet and use descriptive language.
When/Where: Anywhere, anytime. Works well at the beach.

Materials: Paper, pencil or crayons, an alphabet list or 3-D letters, fingers.

The Game: One player uses his imagination to describe a letter, which the second player must guess. For example, Isaac calls out: "What letter looks like two mountains together?" His little brother would be correct if he answered "M!" Then: "What letter looks like two mountains upside down?" "W!" "Right!"

Once the guesser has identified the letter, he writes it down on paper or in the sand. Or have him write in the air, with large motions.

Tips

- If the guesser can't guess the letter, the first player should try to describe it in a different way. Or he could use his finger to write the letter on the guesser's back.
- To make the game easier, lay an alphabet list (see "The Alphabet" in the Appendix) or 3-D letters on the floor or table so that the guesser can see all of the possibilities.

Words All Over Me

Removable tattoos that follow a pattern.

Goals: Practice spelling, rhyming, writing, vocabulary building skills.

Materials: Strips of paper, Post-its, or index cards; adhesive tape; a human body.

When/Where: Anytime, anyplace.

The Game: With your child, make a list of body parts from head to toe. Pick a body part, like the arm, and together, name all the words you can think of that include the same sound: *farm*, *harm*, *alarm*, *charm*, etc. Have him write each word on a separate strip of paper (you can help with spelling if need be) and attach the words to your arm. Move on to the next body part and repeat until you're a walking bulletin board of labels. Then have your child read you all over! (See the following list.)

Variations

■ Time it. See how many words your child can come up within a designated time period.

■ Find objects inside or outside your house to label—a book, lamp, tree, slide, etc.—and attach words that follow the pattern.

■ Have your partner pretend to be asleep and prompt your child to quietly attach words all over him or her.

■ Write and attach words that sound like the body part but do not necessarily follow the spelling pattern. For example, words that rhyme with *eye*—*cry*, *my*, *fly*, *try*, *deny*. (See following list.)

Tips

■ To begin, you might want to limit the game to one or two body parts at a time.

■ Keep a dictionary handy to check spelling or find new words.

■ Start with simple words and work your way up to longer ones.

■ If your child struggles with writing, you can write the words for him and have him copy them.

Words for Words All Over Me

Here are body words to get you started. Once your child gets the hang of this game, have him match spelling or rhyming patterns with words that represent less obvious areas of the body, such as the hair, skin, palm, etc.

Head: *read, behead, dead, lead, bread, dread, spread, thread, tread.* (Rhymes that don't follow the spelling pattern: *bed, said, Ned, fled.*)

Face: *place, grace, disgrace, misplace, lace, race, space, ace, trace.* (Rhymes that don't follow the spelling pattern: *chase, case, base.*)

Eye: *dye, bye, rye, lye.* (Rhymes that don't follow the spelling pattern: *by, buy, cry, die, deny, butterfly, dry, fly.*)

Ear: *fear, near, clear, dear, gear.* (Rhymes that don't follow the spelling pattern: *deer, peer, pier, cheer.*)

Nose: *hose, chose, rose, pose, those, close.* (Rhymes that don't follow the spelling pattern: *goes, oboes, foes, woes, toes, shows, rows, throws.*)

Chin: *bin, twin, thin, spin, shin, win, din.*

Lips: *blips, clips, pips, drips, tips, chips.*

Neck: *check, heck, peck, fleck, wreck, reckless, deck, speck.*

Chest: *best, nest, detest, behest, pester, quest, west, western, Chester.*

Back: *hack, Jack, Mack, shack, pack, whack, black, quack-quack.*

Arm: *farm, alarm, charm, harm.*

Wrist: *twist, resist, persist, insist, fist, twist, mister, sister, grist.*

Hand: *band, bandage, stand, standard, brand, grand, land, bland.*

Finger: *swinger, stinger, singer, linger, lingering.* OR *cling, king, spring, sing, thing, zing.*

Leg: *peg, beg, beggar, Meg, keg.* (Rhymes that don't follow the spelling pattern: *egg.*)

Thigh: *sigh, nigh, high.* (Rhymes that don't follow the spelling pattern: *sky, fly, try, bye, pie.*)

Knee: *flee, bee, fee, wee, tree, gee, see, pee.* (Rhymes that don't follow the spelling pattern: *flea, be, pea, tea, sea.*)

Foot: *soot, took, shook, Nanook, book, nook, good, wood, hood.* (Note: except for *soot*, these words don't rhyme, but they follow the same sound pattern as *foot.*)

Heel: *feel, kneel, peel, eel, wheel, wheelie, steel.* (Rhymes that don't follow the spelling pattern: *steal, real, deal, meal, seal, heal, squeal, Neal.*)

Toe: *doe, Joe, woe, foe, hoe, goes, heroes.* (Rhymes that don't follow the spelling pattern: *dodo, go, no, blow, show, snow, below.*)

Alpha Angels

A new version of a classic childhood activity—with a phonics twist.

Goals: Reinforce the connection between letters and sounds.

Materials: Snow-covered ground or sandy beach.

When/Where: Great for a snowy day or a sunny day at the shore.

The Game: After a good snowfall, dress up warmly and get out into the drifts. Ask your child to think of a letter and draw its shape in the snow either with her whole body, by walking out the letter, or by using a stick. When she's done, have her step away so you can see the letter. If you recognize it, say its name. Ask your child to make its sound or say a word that begins with the letter.

Then it's your turn to make a snow letter for your child to identify.

If you live in a snow-free area, try this game on a sandy beach. In this version, ask your child to build the letter from damp sand.

Variations

- For a challenge, think of a word that begins with the letter. Crown long vowels (like the /ā/ in *apron*) with a stick; top a short vowel (like the /ă/ in *afternoon*) with a pebble. (See "Simple Basic Phonics" in the Appendix.)
- Instead of playing this as a guessing game, you can call out a letter and ask your child to make its shape in the snow or sand.

Tips

- Don't overdo this one—unless your child is having a great time, two or three letters is enough. Leave time to build a snowman or a sandcastle, too.
- Begin with consonants and move to vowels or practice letters that give your child the most trouble.
- If your child can't name or say the sound of the letter, or think of a word, say it for her and have her repeat it.
- Later, over a cup of hot cocoa or ice-cold lemonade, write the letters you made in the snow or sand and words that begin with those letters.

Finger Phonics

For days without snow—a variation on Alpha Angels.

Goals: Reinforce the connection between letters and sounds.

Materials: Fingers.

When/Where: Anytime, anywhere.

The Game: Tell your child you're going to make letters using your fingers—a secret sign language for the alphabet. (See Figure 4.1.) Take turns thinking of letters and making them with your fingers. The player who is not "signing" must guess the letter being made or its sound and then trace its shape in the air with his finger. See which letters you can make using only one hand—like *j* and *o*—and which letters need both hands—like *k* and *z*.

Variations

- Alternate between uppercase and lowercase letters.
- For a more advanced game, each player can spell a word. The other player must guess all the letters and call out the word they spell.

Figure 4.1 *Finger Phonics*

- One player calls out a sound, and the other player must make the corresponding letter with his fingers.
- Go through the alphabet in order, taking turns signing each letter.

Tips

- If your child has trouble visualizing letters, help him write out the alphabet—uppercase and lowercase—to use as a reference.
- If your child has difficulty forming letters with his fingers, you do the signing and have him trace it in the air.
- Have your child sit by your side when you play this game. This is important because, if you sit across from each other, your letter *b* will be reversed and look like a *d* to your child.

Spy Sounds

A guessing game for two senses.

Goals: Reinforce the sounds of letters and develop observation skills.

Materials: None, except a sharp pair of eyes and ears.

When/Where: Anytime, anywhere.

The Game: This variation of the game I Spy uses letter sounds instead of colors. (See "Simple Basic Phonics" in the Appendix.) Player one scans the area for an object and says "I spy with my little eye something that begins with . . . [the sound of the first letter of the object]." Your child must repeat the sound, name the letter, and look for the object that begins with that letter. For example, you spot a robin in the park and say "I spy with my little eye something that begins with *rrrrrrr.*" You can limit the number of guesses or play open-ended. Once player two names the object, it's *her* turn to spy with her little eye.

Variations

- Put two letters together, such as consonant blends like /*bl*/ (as in *blueberry*) or digraphs like /*sh*/ and /*ch*/ (as in *shish kabob* or *child*). (See "Consonant Blends" and "Digraphs" in the Appendix.)
- Use adjectives and nouns instead of sounds, such as "I see a hopping thing with a red breast." (See "Parts of Speech" in the Appendix.)
- Play to practice prepositions: "I spy something that is *on* a table" (or *below, next to, alongside of,* etc.). (See "Parts of Speech" in the Appendix.)
- Don't limit the possibilities to objects you can touch. Think of sky, clouds, breeze.
- For a real challenge, work on end sounds. For example, "I spy something that ends with *rrrrrr*". . . (*car, floor, sister*). Or use a sound from the middle of the word, such as /*b*/ in *robin.*

Tips

- Begin with simple objects and gradually work up to difficult ones.
- Alternate between objects that are easy and difficult to find.
- Have an alphabet chart with pictures available for your child.

Boggling Boggle

Shake up this classic word game for practice in turning letters into words.

Goals: Reinforce letters and their sounds.

Materials: The game Boggle, pencil, and paper.

When/Where: Anytime, anyplace. A good rainy-day game for you and two or more children.

The Game: In the game Boggle, players shake up sixteen alphabet cubes and then, before the timer runs out, have to create as many words as possible using the letters on the face of the cubes. For Boggling Boggle, shake up only five or six letter cubes to start. Player one must identify the letters and think of a word that begins with each letter. Player two then shakes the letters and takes his turn. An adult writes down the words in play if no child is able.

Gradually increase the number of letters being shaken. Or, if your child has mastered beginning sounds, up the ante. Think up words that end in a letter, such as *bug* (if you pick a *g*) or *grab* (if you pick a *b*). On the next round, take away the consonants and focus on short vowels. Work with middle sounds like the /ĕ/ in *bed* or the /ĭ/ in *dip*. (See "Simple Basic Phonics" in the Appendix.)

If you want to make this a competitive game, you can keep score or use the Boggle timer.

Variations

- Ask your child just to name the letters that turn up.
- Have your child rearrange the letters that turn up in alphabetical order, even though some of them will

probably be missing. For example, your child might have only *A*, *C*, *D*, *G*, and *J* to arrange.

■ Think up as many words as possible for each letter.

■ Try to create rhyming words for all the letters that are thrown, such as *boy*, *toy*, and *joy* for the letters *B*, *T*, and *J*.

Tips

■ Make sure you have an alphabet list available. Use one with pictures if your child needs help remembering the sounds of the letters.

■ When it is your turn, use words that expand your child's vocabulary.

■ As your child learns to spell, he can write his word list on his own or spell the words out loud.

Confusing Hopscotch

Jump to clear up the confusion.

Goal: Read the letters *b*, *d*, *p*, and *q* correctly and build memory and coordination.

Materials: Index cards, color markers, four paper plates.

When/Where: Anytime, anywhere you have room to jump around.

The Game: The letters *b*, *d*, *p*, and *q* (see "Tips") look like the same letter facing different directions or turned upside down. When struggling readers encounter words beginning or ending with these letters, they often misread them. For example, they might say *bad* instead of *dad*, *pog* instead of *dog*. This game helps your child tell one letter from the other.

Take twelve index cards. Assign each letter a color: green for *b*, etc. On the first four cards, with your child, write one letter per card in its assigned color. As your child writes, have her name the letters. On the next eight cards, write a series of the colored letters. For example, *b*, *d* on one card, *b*, *q*, *p* on another card, *d*, *q*, *p*, *b* on the third, and so on. The idea is to mix up the number and sequence of the letters on the remaining cards.

Next, on each of the four paper plates, write one confusable letter in its assigned color. Lay the plates on the floor in two rows, with *b* and *d* on top and *p* and *q* underneath. Be sure to have enough space between the plates for your child to jump hopscotch style between them.

Have your child stand before the plates. Now pull a card from the playing deck and call out the letter or letters on the card. Your child must jump on one foot to the appropriate plate or plates. (See Figure 4.2.) If you pull a card with two or more letters, she must jump onto each letter in the order you called. If she is successful, draw the next card and repeat. But if she mishops, read the card again and have her take another try. Continue until all the cards in the deck have been called. Then shuffle the deck and you take a turn jumping as your child reads and calls.

In the next round, pull two cards at a time and read them both. In each successive round, pull an extra card so that the jumper must hop a longer string of letters in a turn. By round four, your child may be jumping *d*, *b*, *q*, *p*, *d*, *b*, *q*, *p*, *d*, *b*, or more.

Figure 4.2 *Confusing Hopscotch*

Variations

- Play this game outside on a sidewalk or in a playground by drawing the letters with sidewalk chalk.

- For a more challenging game, say a word beginning with one of the confusable letters and have your child hop to the correct letter. For example, if the word is *dog*, she hops to *d*; if it is *quit*, she can hop to *q*.

- To up the ante, say words that begin and end with the letters, such as *bad, dab, pad, Deb, bop, blip, quip, blimp*. She must hop to the first target letter she hears, like the *b* in *bad,* and then to the ending letter—the *d*.

- Write vowels on the plates and cards. Call out the short and long vowel sounds and have your child jump to the correct letter. For example, ask her to hop onto the /ŏ/ as in *octopus* and /ō/ as in *open*. (See "Simple Basic Phonics" in the Appendix.)

■ Use confusable words instead of letters. (See "Confusable Words" in the Appendix.)

Tips

■ The letter *q* does not cause struggling readers as much difficulty as the other three confusable letters in words because it is always followed by *u*. But it can be confusing when read as an isolated letter.

Vocabulary and Sight Word Games

 now what these words are? All the words in the preceding sentence are *sight words*, and they should be memorized for instant recognition, because they can't be sounded out. A number of our vocabulary games are devoted to giving children active ways to practice learning these important little words by heart.

Of equal importance are the games in this section that help your child develop a rich spoken vocabulary, which is critical for comprehension. So, when playing them, don't hesitate to expose your child to a plethora of exotic, enticing, and extraordinary words.

Always Remember
- If you see that your child isn't enjoying the game, stop playing. Ask why he didn't like it. Get his ideas about how to make it better.

- At the end of every game, take stock together of the skills you worked on. Be lavish with praise for the things your child did well and be encouraging about the things he found difficult. Be as specific as possible.
- If your child is upset about something that's hard for him to do, remind him of the things he does well. Assure him of your faith in his ability to learn.

Crazy Ates

Turn a family card game into rhyming practice.

Goals: Build vocabulary and practice rhyming and categorizing skills.

Materials: A standard deck of playing cards.

When/Where: Anywhere, anytime, especially when the whole family's in the mood for a card game.

The Game: Shuffle the deck and deal five cards to each player. Put the remaining cards in a stack face down on the table. Start a discard pile by taking the top card from the stack and laying it face up alongside the stack. It's important that you take the first turn.

Follow the basic rules of the classic card game Crazy Eights: that is, each player must lay down a card from his hand that matches the top card in the discard stack either by suit or by number. For example, if the top card is a six of clubs, player one can discard a six of any suit or a club of any denomination.

In Crazy Ates, as player one lays down the first card, he calls out a word—for example, *ate*. Player two must match the new top card in either number or suit and must think up a word that rhymes (*plate*, *crate*, *late*) before he lays down his matching card. (See "Word Families" and "Vowels for Vowel Games" in the Appendix.) If player two has no cards to match, he must pick from the face-down stack until a suitable match is found. As you play, continue to call out words that rhyme with *ate* until an *8* turns up.

Picking an *8* changes everything. The player who has an *8* (of any suit) can lay it on *any* card. At the same time, he can, if he wishes, change the suit (say, from clubs to hearts) *and* change the original word (say, from *ate* to *fun*). Thereafter, players must call out words that rhyme (*run*, *sun*—even *cinnamon bun*) until someone lays down another *8* and changes the word and suit yet again. There are no duplications and no nonsense words allowed—but if your child is having trouble finding a rhyming word, you can help out by giving good hints. A player who cannot come up with a rhyming word must pass. If everyone has exhausted all rhyming possibilities, let your child come up with a new word to rhyme. The first player to get rid of all his cards wins the game.

Throughout the game, keep a running list of the words in play. You can refer to it if your child repeats a word that has already been spoken. However, words that sound alike but are spelled differently (homonyms) are permissible: for example, your child can call out *wait* and *weight* as long as he explains the different meanings. At the end of the game, you can read the whole list together.

Variations

- Play this as a phonics game by announcing a letter and then calling out words that begin with that letter (for example, if *b* is in play, players can call out *boy*, *bat*, *big*, *buffalo*, and so on). As your child gets better at playing, you can practice thinking up words that end with the letter (*rub*, *cab*, *crib*) or that have the letter somewhere inside it (*crabby*, *table*, *Teletubby*).

■ When your child has mastered one thing, aim for something slightly harder. For example, when single consonant sounds become too easy, move on to blends, like the /*bl*/ in *blink*, *blab*, or *blue*. (See "Consonant Blends" in the Appendix.)

■ For an extra challenge, use blends that rhyme, like *blab*, *grab*, *slab*.

Tips

■ If you play this as a phonics game, begin with consonants and move to vowels or practice letters that give your child the most trouble. (See "Simple Basic Phonics" in the Appendix.)

■ If your child can write, ask him to keep the list of words in play. Help him with spelling—especially with variations such as *late*, *weight*, *great*, *wait*.

■ To streamline the game, reduce the size of the deck by removing all cards over *8* before you play.

Set Your Sights

Throwing accurately and reading sight words fluently take lots of practice.

Goals: Read sight words and build eye-hand coordination.

Materials: Index cards or pieces of paper; dark-colored markers; a list of sight words (see "Sight Words" in the Appendix); a Koosh ball, preferably, or something small and easy to toss like a pair of rolled-up socks.

When/Where: Anytime, anywhere you have the space to toss.

The Game: Since sight words cannot be sounded out, repetition is the key to learning them. Throwing is also a skill that needs lots of practice. Even if your child isn't reading correctly or throwing accurately at first, this game will give her the practice she needs to succeed at both skills.

Select ten sight words from a book your child is reading or from "Sight Words" in the Appendix. In large capital letters, write one word on each index card (or spell out the word and let your child write it if her handwriting is legible).

Place the word cards face up on the floor at varying distances from where your child is standing. Make sure the words are easy to read from her spot (if she is small, have her stand on a stool or low chair).

Hand your child the ball. Ask her to toss it onto one of the cards and then read the word. (See Figure 5.1.) If she reads correctly, remove that card, throw the ball back to her, and let her aim for the next word. If your child misreads a word, read it for her and have her repeat. Leave the card on the floor so she can practice reading it again after the other cards have been removed.

If your child misses the target, have her toss again or let her read a word that is closest to where the ball landed. If the ball falls between two words, she must read them both.

On your turn, lay the cards face down. Throw the ball at one of the cards and guess the word you've hit. Ask your child

Figure 5.1 *Set Your Sights*

to turn the card over to see if you guessed correctly. If so, she removes it from play and tosses the ball back to you. If you were wrong, she puts the card back on the floor, face down, before tossing the ball back to you.

Variations

- Place the word cards face down on the floor. When your child hits the word, turn it over.
- Use words that are often confused, such as *what* and *that*, *was* and *saw*. (See "Confusable Words and Letters" in the Appendix.) Make sure you place them a good distance apart from each other.
- Use letters instead of sight words. Your child can either name the letter, make its sound, or say a word that begins with the letter after she throws.
- Use word families or words with blends. (See "Word Families" and "Consonant Blends" in the Appendix.)

■ Write simple math problems on the cards (like
   $2 \times 2 = ?$) or things that have to be memorized, like
   the days of the week or the months of the year.

■ For outside play, use pebbles instead of a ball. Place
   the word cards on the ground and draw a circle in
   the dirt or sand around each one.

Tips

■ If your child can't read a word, don't wait too long to
   read it for her. On the other hand, don't rush to read
   it if she needs a moment to think.

■ Remember to review words that have been mastered.
   Mix these words with new ones your child is
   learning.

Can You Top This?

*A friendly game of one-upmanship can build
vocabulary.*

Goals: Learn synonyms and build vocabulary.

Materials: An active brain and, if handy, a thesaurus.

When/Where: Anyplace, anytime. It's best when the game
emerges naturally from an active situation.

The Game: Keep your eyes open for an opportunity to play.
Suppose you're out with your child on a snowy day. First, ask
him if he knows what a synonym is. If he doesn't, tell him a
synonym is a word that means the same thing as another word.
For example, synonyms for *eat* could be *dine, devour, ingest, con-
sume.* Explain that he can find lots of synonyms in a thesaurus.

Start the game by declaring "My fingers are cold!" Then ask your child to top your statement by finding a synonym for *cold*, such as "My fingers are *freezing!*" You can counter with "My fingers are *frigid!*" which can be topped by "My fingers are *frozen!*" The last person to come up with an appropriate synonym gets to start the next round of play.

If your child's response is not really a synonym, that's fine as long as the word is in the ballpark, such as "My fingers are tingling!" or "My fingers are ice cubes!" However, "My fingers are steaming!" is clearly off the mark. In that case you might gently point out that *steaming* means *hot*—and offer your child another chance to find a word that means about the same thing as *cold*. In the second round, if you wish, you can work on synonyms for *hot*.

If you play this game indoors, keep a list of the synonyms and then look them up in a thesaurus (a good bonus skill) to see if each player's synonym truly matches the original word and to find a lot more synonyms.

Variations

- Play around with similes—phrases, beginning with *like*, that *liken* one thing to another. For example, "My hands are like ice!" can be countered with "My hands are like a glacier!" or "My hands are like the freezer part of the refrigerator!"
- Play around with other parts of speech. (See "Parts of Speech" in the Appendix.) So far you have been playing with adjectives, which are descriptive words. Now find synonyms for verbs (action words). For example, if your child says "Sometimes I yell!" you

might reply "Sometimes I shout!" or "Sometimes I holler!" Or find synonyms for nouns (words for persons, places, or things): "The animal is in the cage" could be countered with "The beast is in the cage" or "The creature is in the cage."

■ Instead of working with synonyms, try a fast-paced version with antonyms, words that mean the opposite of each other. It might go something like this: player one: "My hands are hot!" Player two: "My hands are freezing!" Or, player one: "My hands are wet!" Player two: "My hands are dry!" Or, player one: "My hands are stinky!" Player two: "My hands are fragrant!" And so on.

■ An affectionate variation is to "top" expressions of love: for example, you might say "I love you more than chocolate." Your child might counter with "I love you more than Game Boy." Then you can say "I love you more than eating a box of chocolates in a warm bubble bath," and so on.

Tips

■ If your child can write, have him keep the list of words you've come up with, but help out with spelling if he's having trouble.

■ If your child gets really stuck for a synonym, say one for him and have him repeat it.

■ Write new synonyms that you learn on Post-its and put them up on the refrigerator door. Refer to them as often as possible to reinforce the learning—for example, "Doesn't that strawberry jam smell *fragrant*?"

How Much Is That Word?

Add up the letters and get rich in vocabulary.

Goals: Build vocabulary and, as an added bonus, practice basic addition.

Materials: Index cards; pencils; a favorite children's book, an old magazine, or an old newspaper; a paper bag; a children's dictionary; an alphabet list. (See "The Alphabet" in the Appendix.)

When/Where: At home, preferably with more than two players.

The Game: Assign a dollar value (starting with $1 for *A*, $2 for *B*, $3 for *C*, and so forth) to every letter in the alphabet, ending with *Z* at $26. Write the values next to the letters on your alphabet list. Each player looks at a page from a magazine or a newspaper and copies four or five eye-catching words, one per index card. Put the words in a paper bag and ask your child to shake it up *good*!

Pass the bag around and take turns picking one word (no peeking!). On a separate piece of paper, each player writes the word he picked and the number value for each letter. If she can add up the numbers on her own, she should; if not, help her.

To score, the player must explain what the word means (if she doesn't know, she can ask another player for help or consult the dictionary) and then use it correctly in a sentence. Repeat until all the words have been picked, tallied, and defined. The player who has the most expensive words in all wins the game.

Each time you play, change the value of the letters. For example, you can assign *Z* a $1 value and *A* $26. Or give greater value to vowels or consonants. (See "Simple Basic Phonics" in the Appendix.)

Variations

- If your child picks a word with multiple meanings, offer bonus points if she comes up with one sentence for each definition—for example, "It was a *bright*, sunny day," and "The girl had a *bright* idea."
- If you're on the road, collect words you see on billboards or signs, jot them down, and when you get where you're going, play the game. In a restaurant, you can hunt for the most expensive word on the menu!
- To help your child study for tests, use words from her school spelling and vocabulary lists.

Tips

- If your child can write, have her keep a running list of the words in play. Help her with spelling if she has a hard time.
- Encourage your child to find challenging words in newspapers or magazines—she might even find words that you don't know.
- Use a children's dictionary with large text and simple definitions—but keep an adult dictionary handy, in case someone finds an unusual word.
- Use play money for extra fun.

Room Sleuth

Hear the clues, guess the object.

Goals: Describe and categorize objects, practice listening and observing, and build vocabulary.
Materials: Index cards, markers.

When/Where: At home or in an unfamiliar room—at a friend's house or a hotel.

The Game: Tell your child you are thinking of something in the room. His job is to play detective and find the object.

Describe the function, color, size, or shape of the thing you have in mind. For example, "I'm thinking of something with four legs that sits" (a chair). Your child may ask for more clues or you may provide more descriptive ones, if he has trouble finding the object. If he's making random guesses, repeat the clues.

Once the item is identified, the detective writes its name on a card. Reverse roles, and you become the detective.

When you're done, lay all the cards on a bed or table and see if you can put them in categories. You can sort them by first letter or by the first letter's sound, by color, by function, and so on. How many categories can each object fit into?

Variations

- When you've all gotten good at describing things, make a rule that for a set period of time no one is allowed to use the names of objects in a room—you must refer to them by what they do or what they look like. So, instead of asking someone to turn on the TV, you would say, "Please activate the big black box that transmits moving pictures and sound to the room."

- Add movement to the game. Ask your child to "dance by the long object that looks like you" (the mirror) or "put your foot at the bottom of the object that opens the room to the world" (the door).

Tips

- To expand your child's vocabulary, look for unconventional objects in a room to describe, such as an armoire or an ottoman.
- If an object has more than one name (a sink can also be a basin; a bureau can also be a chest of drawers), write both names on the index card.
- If your child struggles with writing, do the writing for him and have him copy the words.

Odd or Peculiar?

Vocabulary and spelling improve as players decide.

Goals: Build vocabulary and practice spelling and categorizing.
Materials: Pen or pencil, paper.
When/Where: Anytime, anyplace.
The Game: What makes something *odd* and something else *peculiar*? It's a question of spelling. Odd things have double letters, peculiar things don't.

Let your child suggest a category—say, fruit. Begin by asking your child to name all the fruits she can think of. Write them down on a piece of paper. If your child has limited knowledge, help her out. Include some of the more exotic fruits such as mango and pomegranate.

Take another piece of paper and make two columns. Write *ODD* on top of one column and *PECULIAR* on top of the other. The object of the game is to write ten or more pairs of fruit in each column—one with double letters, the other without them. For example, *cherries* go in the *ODD* column; *oranges* belong under *PECULIAR*. (If you run out of odd fruits, remember there are a lot of berries in the world—from blue to goose!)

Ask your child to consult the original list you put together and select one fruit that has a double letter to write under the *ODD* column (apples) and one fruit to write under the *PECU-LIAR* column. Then you take a turn adding a fruit to each column—but to level the playing field, you must do it in your head, without consulting the list.

When you've listed ten ODD/PECULIAR pairs, change categories. (See the following list.) This time you suggest one —say, games: "*Tiddledywinks* are odd, but *checkers* are peculiar" —or animals: "*Giraffes* are odd, but *anteaters* are peculiar."

Eventually you and your child may be able to play this game anywhere, without paper and pencil—just taking turns naming things with double letters and things without. But to begin, it's better to have a list of words your child can consult.

Variations

- Take turns picking the odd word while the other player supplies the peculiar word, then switch.
- You can use this game for all kinds of spelling patterns. For example, if your child's teacher is working on words with two vowels read as the long sound of the first vowel—like the *ea* in *neat* or *seat* or the *oa* in *coat* or *boat*—you can use that as the "ODD" pattern. If you pick food as your category, for example, you might come up with *meat/chicken*, *cream/milk*, or, for double points, *oatmeal/cornflakes*.

(See "Vowels for Vowel Games" and "Word Families" in the Appendix.)

Tips

■ Don't switch to harder phonics patterns until your child has really mastered the double-letter spellings.

■ Try to add atypical words when you're brainstorming your lists. You may be exposing your child to more than just another double-lettered word. If your category is games, for example, has she ever heard of Tiddledywinks or Bottle Caps, and does she know how to play?

ODD or PECULIAR Starter Lists

Fruit

ODD: Apple, cherry, blueberry, gooseberry, blackberry, raspberry, strawberry, currant, lychee, passionfruit

PECULIAR: Orange, peach, papaya, mango, plum, pomegranate, lemon, watermelon, pear, nectarine

Games

ODD: Tiddledywinks, Parcheesi, Scrabble, Gin Rummy, baseball, football, soccer, Hide-and-Seek, chess

PECULIAR: Hopscotch, Old Maid, badminton, Twenty Questions, checkers, hockey, Monopoly, Clue, croquet, miniature golf

Animals

ODD: Kitty, rabbit, moose, goose, meerkat, reindeer, caterpillar, sheep, butterfly, giraffe

PECULIAR: Goat, bear, mule, horse, cow, duck,
centipede, mouse, spider, pig

Vegetables

ODD: Broccoli, beets, cabbages, carrots, eggplants,
green beans, leeks, lettuce, mushrooms, sweet
potatoes

PECULIAR: Cucumber, cauliflower, celery, corn,
jícama, peas, kale, okra, parsnip, spinach

Red Light/Green Light

Run, read, and get to the finish line.

Goals: Learn sight words.

Materials: Markers, paper or cardboard.

When/Where: Outside or in a big indoor space where there
is room to run. Best if played by three or more.

The Game: Make a list of six or seven sight words your child
is having trouble with or is just learning (or see "Sight Words"
in the Appendix). In large letters, write each word on a separate piece of paper.

As in the traditional Red Light/Green Light game, the
caller stands by a tree or wall with his back to the runners, who
stand a good distance away behind a makeshift starting line.
Each runner should be assigned a number. The caller yells out,
"Green light!" and the runners run. As soon as the caller yells,
"Red light!" and turns to face the runners, the runners must
freeze.

In this version, with the runners frozen in place, the caller
holds up a word. Runner number one has five to ten seconds

(the caller silently keeps count) to read it correctly. If he can't, runner number two has five to ten seconds to try. If either one reads the word correctly, everyone takes a step forward. If neither runner can read the word, everyone goes back to the starting line.

The caller turns back to the wall, calling "Green light!" once again, and the runners take off. At the next "Red light!" the caller flashes the next sight word, and runner number three has five to ten seconds to read the word, and so on (make sure every runner gets a turn to read).

Play continues until one of the runners gets close enough to tag the caller. Once the caller is touched, everyone runs back to the starting line as the caller chases them all. If the caller tags someone before he or she reaches the starting line, that person becomes the caller. If no one is tagged, the original caller remains as "traffic cop."

At the end of the game, lay all the words on the ground or floor and read them together. Have the children write in the air the words that they missed.

Variations

- If you have limited space, players can hop or take giant steps instead of run.
- Instead of reading words, players can define words that are held up.
- Play the game to practice spelling. After the caller yells "Red light!" and turns around, he calls out a word that the runner must spell correctly.
- For beginning readers, call out a letter and ask the runner to say its sound and write the letter in the air with her hand.

- To reinforce the alphabet, hold up a letter on a piece of paper. Runners must call out the name of the letter.
- Practice right/left directions. For example, tell runners to touch right hand to left shoulder, right index finger to right knee, and so forth.

Tips

- Remind the players that they are a team and should not laugh at anyone who misses a word. They must work together.
- If the same person has been the caller three consecutive times because he cannot catch the others, have a new traffic cop take over. Everyone should get a chance to run.

The Art in the Article

A treasure hunt for hidden words.

Goals: Recognize compound words and words within words, skim for information, and practice handwriting.

Materials: An old newspaper or magazine, a paper bag, scissors, markers, highlighting pens, a long strip of paper.

When/Where: Anytime, anywhere. Best with more than two players.

The Game: Tape the strip of paper vertically to a wall or to the floor. Ask each player to cut two or three *very* short articles or advertisements out of the magazine or newspaper. Put these clippings in a paper bag and have every player pick out one clipping.

The object is for everyone to peruse his or her article to find big words that have smaller words inside them. As they hunt, players should highlight the words they choose for easy reference. Then everybody takes turns writing the original words and their "hidden words" in a column running down the strip of paper (each player should write his/her initials at the top of the column).

First look for compound words—words made up of two or more complete words—such as *newspaper* or *playground*. Then move on to any word that might have other words hidden inside—such as *out* in *mouth*, *in* in *point*, *tin* in *pointing*, or *a*, *ad*, *is*, *me*, *men* in **advertisement** (even Ent, the tree creatures from *Lord of the Rings*). Players can earn a point for each word-within-a-word spotted.

Variations

- Look only for compound words.
- Play with a time limit.
- Look for words in your child's favorite storybooks.
- Keep a list of all the words you find and see if you can write a story that includes them. (The story can be fanciful, but it has to be logical.)

Tips

- Start with easy-to-read advertisements with big print. Gradually increase the variety and difficulty of the reading material.
- Explain words that your child doesn't know—such as *ilk* in **milk** or *din* or *inner* in **dinner**.
- Play as a group or in teams if your child has difficulty finding the words on his own.

- If writing is difficult for your child, write the original word for him in large letters on the paper strip and ask him to underline or highlight the smaller words he finds.

Packing for Adventure

Be alphabetically prepared for an exciting journey.

Goals: Enrich vocabulary and practice alphabetizing and critical thinking.

Materials: Pencil, lined paper, a dictionary.

When/Where: Anytime, anywhere.

The Game: Is *Robinson Crusoe*—the book or the movie—a family favorite? If your child already knows the story, ask her to retell the beginning—when Robinson was shipwrecked and stranded on a desert island. What if you found yourself in such a predicament? Wouldn't it help to be prepared?

This conversation sets up the game. Ask your child to write the letters of the alphabet in a vertical column along the left side of the lined paper. (See "The Alphabet" in the Appendix.) Then imagine that you have only enough time to fill one large suitcase with up to twenty-six items that you'll need to survive. Set some ground rules for the kind of stuff you can pack: for example, perishables—like milk or eggs— are a no-no, as is anything too big to fit into an average suitcase. Remember that you probably won't have such amenities as electricity or hot and cold running water while you're waiting to be rescued.

Warm up by writing a supply list of possible items to take. Next, players take turns picking an item—either from the supply list or off the top of their head—and writing it next to its corresponding letter on the alphabet list, as shown in the following list (only one item per player per letter, please). You don't have to do this in alphabetical order, but by the end you must fill in all the slots from A to Z.

Once you've compiled your alphabetical supply list, read it together, starting with *A*. Then, decide which of the items to eliminate, for a total of twenty-six. As you compile the final list, any player can think up another, more useful thing to take along—as long as it begins with the same letter of the item you're eliminating.

The object of the game is to create a list of everything you might need in the wild—food, clothes, something to keep you warm and dry, and last but not least, something fun to read. You'll find that some items will need to be paired with others to be of use: for example, if you take a *flashlight* or a *Game Boy*, you'll need *batteries*—which means you may have to rule out *books*! If you've filled the *T* slot with *tunafish*, you have no room for a *tent*, and you'll definitely need a *knife* or a *can opener*! Choosing the right item to take with you requires critical thinking.

Here's an example of a list that needs to be pared down to one item per letter:

apples or *applesauce*
batteries or *books* or *ball*
crackers or *candles*
dates or *dominoes*
earmuffs or *eating utensils*
flashlight or *freeze-dried food*
galoshes or *guitar* or *Game Boy*
hammer or *hats* or *Huckleberry Finn*

iodine or *ink*
jelly or *juice*
knives or *kitchenware*
lanterns or *lemons*
medicines or *matches*
nuts or *navel oranges*
oatmeal or *overcoats*
pots or *peanut butter*
quilts or *Q-tips*
radio or *rope*
sweaters or *Swiss Army knife*
tent or *tunafish* or *toys*
underwear or *umbrellas*
volleyballs or *vitamins*
water or *watches*
xylophone or *x-ray glasses* or *X-Men figures*
yams or a *yo-yo*
zinc oxide or *zucchini*

Variations

- Hunt through the dictionary for things that make sense to include in your survival kit.
- Allow two items for each letter instead of one (in which case you'll need a bigger suitcase).
- Turn the game into a treasure hunt: find twenty-six alphabetic things in your house and fill a real suitcase (and then put them back!).
- Pack for a trip to an imaginary planet.
- Pack only items in a particular category, such as twenty-six food items or twenty-six books or twenty-six articles of clothing.

Tips

- Allow double words if they are appropriate—such as *inflatable raft* or *calamine lotion*—or book titles like *Black Beauty* or *Harry Potter*.
- Allow the use of brand names—like *Gatorade* or *Game Boy*. Point out that these are proper nouns, which are capitalized, unlike common nouns—like *soft drink* or *video game*, which are not. (See "Parts of Speech" in the Appendix.)
- If your child can't think of an item, remind her of the basic necessities—food, clothing, material for shelter—and her favorite books!
- If the thought of being stranded disturbs your child, approach this as a planning list for an extended trek into the wild.

Fishing for Words

Don't let the big words get away! Fish for new vocabulary.

Goals: Build vocabulary, read sight words, and build eye-hand coordination.

Materials: Small magnets, string or lanyard, index cards, markers, paper clips, a plastic bucket.

When/Where: Anytime, at home or outside when there's no wind.

The Game: Make a fishing pole by tying a long piece of string around a magnet. For a touch of realism, cut the index cards into fish shapes, but make sure there is enough room to write on them.

Pick ten words from your child's vocabulary or spelling list or from a book she's reading. Review the words and their definitions. Write one word per index card and put this stack of word cards aside. Then write the definition of each word on a separate index card and set the definition pile aside as well.

Attach a paper clip to each word card and spread them out face down on the floor. Ask your child to *catch* one of the words with her fishing pole. She must read it and give its definition. If she reads and defines the word correctly, put the card in the bucket. If she cannot read the word, read it for her, discuss its meaning, and ask her to use it in a sentence. Then "throw the fish back" by laying the card face down again. Now you take a turn.

Once all the word cards have been put in the bucket, attach paper clips to the definition cards and lay them out on the floor. This time each player must catch and read a definition and state the word it defines. Again, do the reading if your child is struggling.

Variations

- After your child catches a word, give her four possible definitions and have her select the correct one.
- Lay all the word and definition cards face up. Fish for the word card, then catch its definition as well.
- Fish for sight words. (See "Sight Words" in the Appendix.) Lay the cards face down and have her read what she catches. Or place the cards face up and ask your child to catch a particular sight word, for example, the *what* fish or the *went* fish.
- For some phonics practice, fish for letters to reinforce letter sounds. (See "Simple Basic Phonics" in the

Appendix.) Write letters on the cards. Ask your child to catch the letter that sounds like /d/ as in *dolphin*. Or practice middle or end sounds by fishing for the /k/ in *trunkfish* or the /p/ in *shrimp*.

■ Use more difficult sounds—digraphs and diphthongs—such as /sh/ for *shark* or /st/ for *stingray*. (See "Digraphs" in the Appendix.)

■ With beginning readers, fish for individual letters. Or fish for letters that spell simple words, like *C-A-T*.

■ Fish for math practice. Put math problems on the cards and have your child supply the answer for what she catches.

■ For spelling practice, have your child catch a word from her spelling list, read it out loud, then turn the card over and spell the word correctly.

Tips

■ Along with some challenging words, be sure to include words your child already knows or you feel will be easy for her. If every word is a struggle to read or define, she will quickly lose interest in the game.

Dictionary Snack

A rainy-day family game—with a delicious reward.

Goals: Use a dictionary, alphabetize, practice spelling, and build vocabulary.

Materials: A children's dictionary; Scrabble tiles or index cards with letters of the alphabet; paper; pen, pencils, or crayons; three bowls; M&Ms, pretzels, popcorn, or other finger food.

When/Where: Home—best with the whole family.

The Game: Empty the snack into one bowl. Separate letter tiles or index cards into consonants and vowels. (See "Simple Basic Phonics" in the Appendix.) Put the consonants face down in the second bowl, the vowels face down in the third bowl. Player one picks one vowel and one consonant. The player must then put the two letters together in any order and find a word in the dictionary that begins with that letter combination. Once he finds a word, the player reads it (or if the word is too long or difficult, has someone else read it)—and gets a point and a snack.

For an extra point (and an extra snack), the player defines the word—in his own words. For yet another point and snack, he uses the word in a sentence. At the end of his turn, the player writes the word he found on a piece of paper, initials it, and adds the points he's earned. Then he passes the paper to the next person, who takes a turn.

If your child loves the thrill of winning, you can tally up points at the end of the game, using the initialed word list. But in truth everybody wins, because learning how to use the dictionary is the reward!

Variations

- As your child's reading ability improves, you can complicate the game. For example, specify "only compound words"—that is, words made up of two words, like *newspaper*, *cowboy*, and *cowgirl*.

- As a bonus, have everybody make up a sentence or a story using all the words on the list at the end of the game.

Tips

- Don't play this game right before a big meal!
- If your child has difficulty with alphabetical order, have a copy of the alphabet handy. (See "The Alphabet" in the Appendix.)
- If your child isn't used to consulting a dictionary, it may take him some time to find a word. Be patient. This is a difficult skill to grasp, but it's worth the time invested. As his skill increases, you can experiment with time limits.

Sight Word Suicide

Little brother Emmett's version of the schoolyard game: read the word and race to the wall.

Goals: Recognize sight words, build eye-hand coordination, and practice throwing and catching a ball.

Materials: Paper, strong tape, markers or sidewalk chalk, a ball, a wall, a referee's whistle.

Where/When: In a playground with handball courts or against a garage door or a wall. This game is most fun when played with three or more children.

The Game: Begin with ten sight words, or words that cannot be sounded out, such as *of, to, was, where*. (See "Sight Words" in the Appendix.) In large letters, write one word on each page and tape all ten pages to the wall a good distance apart from each other (or write the words in chalk on the wall, leaving a lot of space between words).

Player one throws the ball at one of the ten words on the wall. As soon as the ball hits the word, player one must read it (a grown-up referee makes sure the word is read correctly). Anyone but the thrower can catch this ball on the rebound, throw the ball at another word, and read it.

However, if the thrower *misreads* the word, the referee blows the whistle and calls out the correct word. When the whistle is blown, everyone races to the wall. The first player to touch the word gets a chance to read it. If she reads it correctly, she gets the next throw. If not, the referee reads the word and sends everyone back to the starting line. The referee then tosses the ball to a different player, who must aim for a new word. Play continues until all ten words have been read correctly. Then another round begins, with ten new words.

If a child has trouble hitting a particular word, she must read the word closest to where the ball lands. If it falls between two words, she must read them both. If the ball lands nowhere near a word, the referee blows the whistle and calls out a word posted on the wall. The first player to touch the word gets the next throw.

Variations

- Put ten letters on the wall. Players must hit a letter and then say the letter's name and/or a word that begins with that letter.
- Use only words your child confuses, like *of* and *for*, *from* and *form*, *they* and *their*. (See "Confusable Words and Letters" in the Appendix.)
- For older children, adapt the game to help study for a math test. For example, on the wall, post $9 \times 1 = ?$,

$9 \times 2 = ?$ and so on. The thrower must call out the answer to the problem he hits with the ball.

Tips

■ It doesn't matter if your child hits the target, though she should try. What's most important is practice in reading sight words. Since you cannot sound out these words, repetition is essential to learning them.

■ Use words from your child's spelling lists or pull them from books she is reading. When you read with your child, make a note of the words she stumbles over to post the next time you play.

■ When posting the words on the wall, make sure you put a lot of distance between confusable words like *what* and *that*, *wish* and *which*, *want* and *what*, etc.

Fore and Aft

Use prefixes and suffixes to guess a player's word while you stick up his body.

Goals: Learn prefixes and suffixes and their meanings, build vocabulary, and read multisyllabic words.

Materials: Index cards, two different-colored pens or markers, tape, a children's dictionary.

When/Where: Anywhere, anytime.

The Game: Explain to your child what prefixes and suffixes are: little add-ons to the main part, or root, of words that change or qualify the meaning of the word. (See "Prefixes, Suffixes, and Roots" in the Appendix.) Prefixes pop up at the beginning of root words, such as *re-* in *redo, retell, rewrite* (where *re-* means "to do something again"). Suffixes are added to the end of root words, such as the powerful *-s*, which turns a single item into more than one (would you rather have a dollar or dollar*s* in your pocket?)

Choose three prefixes and three suffixes from the list in the Appendix. With your child, print each one in large letters on a separate index card—the prefixes in one color (say, red), the suffixes in another (say, blue). Make sure the prefixes are followed by a hyphen (like this: *RE-*) and that the suffixes are preceded by a hyphen (like this: *-S*).

As you write, talk about their meanings. Then come up with a list of twelve words—two for each prefix and suffix. For instance, if you choose the prefix *un-*, which means "not," you might list two of these: *unhappy, undo, unsure,* or *uninterested*. If you pick the suffix *-ful,* which means "full of," your word list might include two of these: *wonderful, joyful, thankful,* or *wishful*.

Put the word list where both players can see it. Shuffle the index cards and deal, face down, one to your child and one to yourself. Then, with a piece of tape, fasten *your* card to your child's body. The card must be attached *so that it cannot be read,* on the forehead if it's a prefix or on the back if it's a suffix.

Next, silently pick a word from the word list that includes the prefix or suffix, which is now "stuck" on your child. For example, if he's sporting the *un-* prefix, you might choose *undo* from the list. Then offer clues to the word, such as "It's what you do to your shoelaces when you need to take off your shoes."

Your child gets two guesses to figure out the word, referring to the word list if need be. If his guess is correct, he can unstick the index card from his forehead and set it aside. If not, you should remove the card, reveal your word, and talk about its meaning. Then replace the card in the deck to be replayed later.

Then it's your child's turn to stick his prefix/suffix index card on *you*, pick a suitable word from the word list, and offer clues. If he isn't sure about what's written on his card, remind him that a prefix is followed by a hyphen and goes on the forehead; the suffix starts with a hyphen and goes on the back.

To level the playing field, you can get one guess. If you're wrong, or if your child gave inaccurate clues, talk about the word and its meaning and return the card to the deck.

One player should tick off the words from the word list as they are guessed, indicating the guesser by his initials. At the end of the round, the person who has correctly guessed the greatest number of words gets to be dealer and *re*shuffle the deck.

Variations

- If this is difficult for your child, work with one prefix and one suffix at a time and list very simple words.

- For more of a challenge, require that each player guess the secret word *and* explain the meaning of the prefix or suffix.

- Instead of choosing a word from the list, the guesser can say the meaning of the prefix or suffix (for example, if your opponent says "It's a suffix that means "without something," you might guess the card says -*less*, as in *hopeless* or *clueless*).

- Make up nonsense words using prefixes and suffixes. For example, if you've been working on -*vore*, which means "eater of," in words like *omnivore*, *herbivore*, or *carnivore*, someone might propose *bananavore* or *cocoavore*.

Tips

- If your child finds this difficult at first, play open-ended: give more hints and allow an unlimited number of guesses until he thinks of the word.
- Use the dictionary to help you find good words—and don't forget to read the meanings of the prefixes, suffixes, and roots.

6

Comprehension Games

 he best way to help your child really comprehend what she's reading is by reading a lot and talking a lot about what you're reading together.

As a supplement to all that great reading, the games in this section focus on specific comprehension strategies that come automatically to good readers: following the sequence of a story, understanding the difference between the story's main ideas and supporting details, and more.

Always Remember

■ If you see that your child isn't enjoying the game, stop playing. Ask why she didn't like it. Get her ideas about how to make it better.

■ At the end of every game, take stock together of the skills you worked on. Be lavish with praise for the things your child did well and be encouraging about the things she found difficult. Be as specific as possible.

■ If your child is upset about something that's hard for her to do, remind her of the things she does well. Assure her of your faith in her ability to learn.

Instant Replay

Retelling a story in your own words is a sign that you understand what you just read.

Goals: Comprehend a story and its sequence of events.
Materials: A book and stepping-stones made out of sturdy paper plates, real stones, or seashells.
When/Where: At home, at the beach, on a playground, at a picnic.
The Game: On the floor or ground, lay out a bunch of stepping-stones, about a foot apart. Put a treat on the final plate as a reward.

Find a story or part of a story and have your child read it to you. If he is struggling, read it to him. Then ask him to retell it in his own words while leaping from stone to stone. (See Figure 6.1.) Each stone represents the next part of the story. Your child may need time to rest on a stone as he thinks through what happened next.

If your child leaves out an important point in the story, misunderstands something in the reading, or tells the story in

Figure 6.1 *Instant Replay*

the wrong order, gently get him back on track by rereading the sentence or paragraph he omitted, misplaced, or misunderstood. Have him go back to the first stone and start again. The idea is to retell the story correctly and get to the final stone, where the reward is waiting! Then it's your turn to retell and step.

Variations

- For an extra challenge, try to tell the story (and take the steps) backward. (Imagine starting with the wolf falling down the chimney at the brick house of the third little pig!)
- You can play this with a ball instead of plates. Toss the ball back and forth while your child retells the story. Or let him toss it against the wall. See how

long you can keep the ball in play while retelling the
story.

Tips

- Keep extra plates on hand for a long, complicated tale.
- Start with very short stories or one or two paragraphs.
  Work up to longer material.
- If your child is making a lot of mistakes, consider
  picking a simpler or shorter story until next time. Or
  take a break and come back to the original story.
- If your child gets bogged down in detail, ask him to
  think of the most important events, or he'll run out
  of plates.

What Do You Know?

*The more we read, the more we know. The more we
know, the more we read.*

Goals: Build general knowledge to improve reading comprehension and practice skimming, categorizing, and distinguish-
ing fact from opinion.

Materials: Pencil; index cards; a die; a newspaper or magazines; and a dictionary, an atlas, an almanac, and/or a children's
encyclopedia.

When/Where: Anytime, anywhere.

The Game: Give each player a section of the newspaper or a
magazine and allow everyone time to skim through it. From
headlines or articles, players are to find three words naming one
person, one place, and one thing and write each on a separate
index card. To help the younger player or nonreader, read the

headline out loud and have her identify the person, place, or thing.

Collect the cards, shuffle, and place them face down on the table. Player one (best if an adult, to model how to play the game) picks a card and throws the die. The number that turns up is the number of things the player must state about the person, place, or thing on the face of the card.

For example, if the first index card says *Hero* and the die turns up on number three, player one must state three things she knows about heroes ("They're fearless, they rescue people or animals, they can be men or women"). If player two rolls a four and turns up a card that says *Canada*, he might say "It's in North America, it's a neighbor of the United States, some people speak French there, and it has moose."

If the player comes up with the full number of details dictated by the roll of the die, she earns a point for each one. If she can't state the full number indicated by the die, any other player can supply information to complete the number of facts required—not to earn points, just to be helpful.

The details can be obvious or little known, but they must be true. Any facts that sound questionable—for example, that the president has green eyelashes—can be challenged by any player and checked for accuracy in a dictionary, encyclopedia, or atlas.

Variations

- Play as a group or in teams, with everybody brainstorming as much as they can about the subject on the index card.
- Search only for names of famous people or favorite TV or book characters (like Stuart Little).

- Skim for people, places, or things in the dictionary rather than the newspaper. Point out that the *n* next to a word tells you it's a noun. (See "Parts of Speech" in the Appendix.)

Tips

- Help your child skim the paper or magazine by showing how you do it. You can use a highlighting marker, if you wish, to mark the people, places, and things you find.
- Encourage the use of reference books.
- Keep track of the things your child takes interest in or knows little about and buy or borrow books or videos on those subjects.

Writing, Writing Everywhere

A treasure hunt yields a smorgasbord of writing styles.

Goals: Identify and categorize different forms of written materials.

Materials: A big box, lots of Post-its, pens or markers.

When/Where: Anywhere, anytime. Works best with at least three players.

The Game: Begin by asking your child to think of all the different types of writing in the world. How many can he name? Start the thinking process by mentioning nursery rhymes or fairy tales, poems or songs. Keep expanding the idea of writing: a menu, a postcard, an E-mail, a candy bar wrapper—anything with words on it.

Put a big box on the kitchen table. Set a time limit—from ten minutes to an hour. The idea of the treasure hunt is for everybody to search the house and collect different kinds of writing—the zanier the better—to add to the box. A sharp-eyed player might contribute game instructions, a coupon, his favorite book, a cereal box. Players should attach a Post-it with their name on it to each object they find.

When time is up, assemble all the players and go through the box together, categorizing the samples you find. For example, all menus go together, as do all promotional flyers—or fortune cookie fortunes. Talk about the ways each writing sample is different—why poetry, say, is not written the same way as a newspaper ad. Tally up each player's contributions and, if you wish, give a prize to the one who has the most variety.

Variations

- Restrict your hunts to certain categories, such as food—recipes, nutrition labels, packaging materials, menus—or animals: stories, pet adoption ads, poems, pet food labels.
- Stretch your time limit to a day or two and let players look for samples outside the house (at school, at the supermarket).
- Turn this into a writing game by using the samples as models to create your own menu, flyer, poem, etc.

Tips

- It really helps to brainstorm a wide range of different styles of writing before the hunt.
- You can play in teams if this game is difficult for your child to do alone.

Exploding Story

Put a story back together—and find out what's important.

Goals: Comprehend story sequence and pick out important events or the main idea.

Materials: Story or chapter book, index cards, markers or pens.

Where/When: Anyplace, anytime. A good rainy day game or backyard game.

The Game: Have your child read a story or chapter to you. If he's having trouble, read it to him or take turns reading. When you're finished, ask him to retell the important events of the story in his own words, one event at a time. Write each event on an index card until you have recorded the beginning, middle, and end of the story.

Give the cards to your child and ask him to "explode the story" by throwing them in the air. (See Figure 6.2.) Ask him to put the index cards back in their proper order on the floor. If your child cannot read, or is having trouble reading, read the cards to him and have him tell you the proper order. Save the deck so you can explode this story another time.

Variations

- Use an egg timer to see how fast the story can be put back together.
- As your child progresses, choose longer and more detailed stories.
- Try reassembling the index cards in different ways and see what happens (for example, tell the story backward or start in the middle).

Figure 6.2 **Exploding Story**

- If your child cannot read, have her illustrate the index cards—she can use the pictures as guides after she explodes the story.
- Try to explode a poem.

Tips

- Start with a simple story or one your child knows well such as "The Three Little Pigs."
- Prompt your child to reread the story if he is unsure of the sequence.
- Help your child avoid getting bogged down by unimportant details by asking questions. For example, "Which is more important, that Red Riding Hood goes to visit her grandmother or that she has yellow hair?"

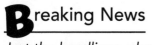reaking News

Just the headlines, please.

Goals: Practice summarizing, identify the main idea of a story or event, recognize a person's point of view, and practice writing skills.

Materials: Pens or pencils, three-hole blank paper to write the "Family News," a three-ring binder.

When/Where: Anywhere, for three or more players. A great game for mealtime.

The Game: On TV, news announcers have only a few minutes—sometimes a few seconds—to communicate the main points of an important event. In this game players challenge each other to come up with the shortest version of an event, an experience, or a story.

Player one begins by recounting something that happened to her during the day or week. When she's finished, player two has to create a "headline"—that is, summarize the story in the shortest possible way. Any other player (including the original storyteller) can then try to condense the "headline" even more.

For example, imagine that a child made a mess in his room and that his mother yelled at him and made him clean it up. Mom can tell the story of how much of a mess he made, including all the gory details—dirty socks under the bed, a damp towel on the floor, toys strewn all over, etc.—and how mad she got. A player could sum it all up in one headline: "MOM REALLY HITS THE ROOF ABOUT DIRTY ROOM!" Another player could come up with something a little shorter: "MOM BLOWS GASKET IN DIRTY DIGS!" The winning player would produce the shortest of all: "MOM

ON MESS RAMPAGE!" Then the next player takes a turn telling a story.

The person who expresses an event accurately in the shortest possible way gets to have her headline included in the day's edition of the "Family News." (The editor-in-chief—a grown-up—can date and write the headlines on a piece of three-hole paper, to be kept in a binder.) You can read all the headlines a few months later and see if you can recall what the fuss was all about.

Variations

- Require the headline to be a complete sentence: for example, "MOM ON MESS RAMPAGE" would need a verb and an article (see "Parts of Speech" in the Appendix)—"MOM *GOES* ON *A* MESS RAMPAGE!"

- Write alternate headlines about the same event but with a different slant: for example, if you want to emphasize the outcome of Mom's rampage, try "JOHNNY CLEANS UP!"

- If the event involved two or more members of the family, get all sides of the story and create multiple headlines from each person's point of view. For example, the alleged messer-upper could state his version of events: "BOY FALSELY ACCUSED OF MAKING A MESS" or "MYSTERY MESS BLAMED ON FUGITIVE SON" or "BOY: 'I DIDN'T DO IT!'" Post the headlines stating both sides of the story in the "Family News" for that date.

- Help your child write a short paragraph about the event under the headline, incorporating the five

*W*s—who, what, where, when, why (See Squeaky-Clean Tales on page 119)—and add the paragraph to your news sheet.

■ Illustrate the headlines.

■ Create a special Travel Edition of "Family News" when you're on vacation—with a photo spread and captions.

Tips

■ Design your own "Family News" masthead and make copies of blank pages with decoration printed on top. Add a catchy slogan like *All the News That's Fit for Us!* Keep a supply of pages handy for writing down the headlines.

Lunchbox Surprise

It's fun to get adjectives with your peanut butter sandwich.

Goals: Use adjectives, build vocabulary, decipher clues, and practice predicting.

Materials: Index cards or colorful paper, markers, a lunchbox, a planned menu for the family meal.

When/Where: For school or camp days.

The Game: If you prepare lunch for your child to take to school or camp, this is a perfect game that can last for five whole days.

First, decide what you're going to serve for dinner that night. For example, imagine that you plan to make spaghetti and meatballs, salad, and chocolate pudding.

Next, make a list of adjectives (see "Parts of Speech" in the Appendix) that describe the foods you'll be serving. *Long*, *white*, and *floppy* might describe the spaghetti. *Round* and *tasty* are adjectives that can apply to meatballs—or, if you really want to give a hint, try *meaty*. Do the same for the salad (*green*, *leafy*) and the pudding (*brown*, *slippery*, and *sweet* might do unless yours is *lumpy*). And don't forget the *rich*, *red* tomato sauce.

Finally, write the adjectives on an index card or colorful piece of paper. Tuck the card into your child's lunchbox. The words are clues: by the time your child comes home from school, she should have figured out the whole meal either by herself or with the help of someone who can read. If she has trouble reading a word, or she doesn't understand what it means, show her when you sit down to dinner. ("The lettuce in this salad has green leaves; that's why it's leafy!")

Variations

- Before the meal, collect the adjectives and, together, write a menu that incorporates them: main course— tasty meatballs, floppy spaghetti, red tomato sauce; side dish—leafy green salad; dessert—sweet, slippery brown pudding.

- The adjectives don't always have to describe food. They can also describe a fun activity you're planning for after school or the weekend. If you're going to the beach, for example, the clues could be *wet* and *salty* for the water and *dry* and *grainy* for the sand.

- You can simply include a note that says "I love you because you're . . ." and fill in the blanks with flattering adjectives. This is not a game, but the note should make your child smile.

Tips

- Always refer to the descriptive words as adjectives, but don't correct your child if she doesn't use that word. If she keeps hearing you say "adjective" often enough, sooner or later she'll catch on.
- Try to make the adjectives progressively harder and longer—*crimson* for the tomato sauce, *entangled* for the spaghetti.

Sequence Scramble

Emmett's game of unscrambling a series of events and putting them in the proper order.

Goals: Practice sequencing, sentence structure, and listening.
Materials: Nothing but a nimble brain; paper and pencil optional.
When/Where: Anytime, anywhere. Good to play at bedtime or in the car.
The Game: Tell your child that *you* are going to scramble up a list of the things you did that day and *she* is going to put them in correct order. Pick three or four activities to start with and gradually increase the number of events to put in sequence. You might begin: "Today we went to the playground, got dressed, ate dinner, and woke up." Once she puts the events in order, she can give you a scramble to undo.

As your child gets better at sequencing, read or tell a short, familiar story out of sequence and see if she can straighten things out. For example, did the Big Bad Wolf first blow down the house of bricks or the house of sticks?

Variations

- Ask your child to scramble some things she did at school that day for you to put in the right order. She'll enjoy correcting you if you get things wrong. Plus, this is a good way to get more than "Nothing" as an answer when you ask what happened at school.

- Scramble/unscramble a sentence, such as "Boy the went for shopping skateboard a new."

- If your child can read, scramble/unscramble a simple recipe from the side of a favorite food box—say, of macaroni and cheese or rice. Cut up the various instructions, scramble, and have your child reassemble them.

- For beginning readers, use tactile letters or numbers, mix them up in a bag, and have your child put them in sequential order.

- Mix up photographs from a family outing for your child to arrange in chronological order. (You can write captions, too! See "Caption It" on page TK.)

Tips

- If your child has trouble recalling what you said, write down the events—out of order, of course. The point of the game is sequencing, not remembering. As your child gets better at the game, his memory will improve.

- When it's your child's turn to scramble, remind her to stick to the most important events, not to get bogged down in details.

Which Way to Go?

Connecting words, like road maps, point to a certain direction.

Goal: Understand connecting words and how they signal meaning or which way a sentence is headed, practice writing.

Materials: Different-colored markers, index cards, a long piece of paper.

When/Where: Anytime, anywhere.

The Game: Select one connecting word from each of the four categories below (*Plus*, *Contradiction*, *For Example*, and *Explanation*). Assign a different color to each type of word and write each on an index card:

> **and** (a Plus word that indicates "I have other things to say");
>
> **but** (a *Contradiction* word that indicates "there's another side to the story");
>
> **such as** (a *For Example* word that tells you specific examples will follow); and
>
> **because** (an Explanation word that leads to the reason you said or did or thought something).

Together, think up a short, simple sentence—for example, "I like video games." Write it on the first line of the paper. Mix up the index cards and put them on the table, face down in a pile. The idea of the game is to pick a card and then change the original sentence using the connecting word. Keep going until you've picked all four cards. Then mix up the deck again, write another short sentence, and play another round. When the ideas come easily to your child, pick four more connecting words from the list below.

For example, if player one turns up an *and* card, he could say and write "I like video games AND I love to play them with my friends." If player two picks a *but*, he might say and write "I like video games, BUT I like movies better." (And so on: "I like video games SUCH AS *Spider-Man*" or ". . . BECAUSE they're fun to play.")

After you've created a new sentence, write it underneath the original one and set the card aside for round two.

Variations

- Instead of writing declarative sentences—sentences that make a statement—you can try questions, which are somewhat harder. ("Did she go downtown BECAUSE she had to stop by the library AND return the books?") (See "The Basic Sentence" in the Appendix.)

- Up the ante by requiring the use of two (or more) connecting words in a sentence. For example, start with "Mary ate fried chicken AND potato salad, BUT she didn't eat her carrots." Then see how far you can go—"Mary eats fried chicken AND potato salad, BUT she doesn't eat vegetables, SUCH AS broccoli, BECAUSE she really hates green food."

- Play the game verbally, as follows: player one *calls out* a sentence ("She went downtown"), player two picks a card and modifies the sentence accordingly ("She went downtown BECAUSE she had to buy a new skateboard"). Then it's player two's turn to call out a new sentence for the other players to extend.

Tips

- To hold your child's interest, begin with sentences concerning things he enjoys or has strong feelings about. For example: "My brother watches television shows AND . . ." or "We hate going to school BECAUSE . . ."

■ The sentences can be as long as you wish, as long as they make sense. Part of the fun is to see how much you can stretch an original thought, using connecting words to keep you going.

■ If your child does the writing, encourage him to use his best handwriting or cursive writing.

Connecting Words (Conjunctions)

Plus Words ("I have something more to say")

    too
    also
    next
    furthermore

Contradiction Words ("There's another side to the story")

    although
    rather
    on the contrary
    instead of

For Example Words ("Specific examples will follow")

    for example
    for instance
    similar to
    like

Explanation Words ("Here's the reason for something")

    for
    so that
    because
    in order to

lizabethan Insults

Let these bawdy insults fly.

Goals: Enrich vocabulary, practice handwriting, identify adjectives and nouns.

Materials: A list of insults from the time of Queen Elizabeth I of England (1558–1603) (following), index cards, pens or markers.

When/Where: Anytime, anywhere. Best with more than two players.

The Game: This game may disintegrate into bawdy name calling. But since most people today would not be offended if they're called a "saucy, earth-vexing apple-john," you and your child can focus on the rich descriptive nature of the words that were so offensive oh-so-many years ago.

With your child, look over the insult list. Explain that the first two columns contain adjectives (words that describe nouns) and the last column is a list of nouns (usually, persons, places, or things, but in this case, nasty names for persons). (See "Parts of Speech" in the Appendix.)

Together, select ten words from each column and write each word on a separate index card. As you write, read the words aloud and review which ones are adjectives and which are nouns.

Mix up the cards (adjectives with nouns) and place them face down in one pile on a table. Deal three cards to each player. The object is to make a complete insult—two adjectives and one noun.

If player one is lucky enough to have been dealt a complete insult, she lays her three cards face up on the table in proper order (adjective, adjective, noun), then reads the insult, with feeling, to the player on her left: for example, "You artless, clapper-clawed, clotpole!" She may then draw three new cards from the face-down stack.

However, if she is holding only three adjectives (or three nouns), she must pick a card from the face-down stack, then discard one from her hand into a discard pile, face up. If the next player doesn't have a complete insult in *his* hand, he can either pick a card from the discard pile or from the new card pile. If that card supplies the missing part of speech, the player lays down his cards and insults the person to his left. And so it goes. At no time may a player hold more than three cards after discarding.

If any player lays out her cards in an improper order (say, "clotpole, artless, clapper-clawed!"), she loses her turn. If the player on the left can rearrange the insult correctly, he can say it back to her. Continue playing until all the cards have been picked up. Next time you play, use thirty different words.

Variations

- When you hurl your insults, replace *you* with *thou* for more Elizabethan flavor—explaining that *thou* is an archaic form of *you*.
- Place two piles of cards face down on the table, one pile of adjectives and one of nouns, and roll a die. The number a player rolls determines the number of adjectives that she must select, plus one noun. If a player rolls a six, she must pull six adjectives and one noun. She then places the cards face up and reads the insult, beginning the sentence with *you* or *thou*:

"Thou currish, rank, rude-growing, full-gorged, gleeking, impertinent pumpion!"

■ Players must first put the adjectives in alphabetical order ("Thou currish, full-gorged, gleeking, impertinent, rank, rude-growing pumpion!")

■ Take the list and randomly read from it, selecting one from each column. This isn't a game per se, but it's lots of fun.

■ See if you and your child can invent your own insults. Isaac once called his brother "You war-pigged, bad-breathed, fish-smelling, apple-john!"

■ After the game, see how many of the insulting adjectives or nouns you can find in an adult dictionary. Just what *is* an apple-john anyway?

Tips

■ If your child cannot read, you can work as a team, and you can do the reading for her. See if she can identify which words are describing words (adjectives) and which ones are persons, places, or things (nouns).

■ Even if your child can read the words, you should help her with the more difficult pronunciations.

Elizabethan Insult Lists

Adjective	Adjective	Noun
artless	base-court	apple-john
bawdy	bat-fowling	baggage
beslubbering	beef-witted	barnacle
bootles	beetle-headed	bladder
churlish	boil-brained	boar-pig
cockered	clapper-clawed	bugbear

Adjective	Adjective	Noun
clouted	clay-brained	bum-bailey
craven	common-kissing	canker-blossom
currish	crook-pated	clack-dish
dankish	dismal-dreaming	clotpole
dissembling	dizzy-eyed	coxcomb
droning	doghearted	codpiece
errant	dread-bolted	death-token
fawning	earth-vexing	dewberry
fobbing	elf-skinned	flap-dragon
forward	fat-kidneyed	flax-wench
frothy	fen-sucked	flirt-gill
gleeking	flap-mouthed	foot-licker
goatish	fly-bitten	ustilarian
gorbellied	folly-fallen	giglet
impertinent	fool-born	gudgeon
infectious	full-gorged	haggard
jarring	guts-gripping	harpy
loggerheaded	half-faced	hedge-pig
lumpish	hasty-witted	horn-beast
mammering	edge-born	hugger-mugger
mangled	hell-hated	joithead
mewling	idle-headed	lewdster
paunchy	ill-breeding	lout
pribbling	ill-nurtured	maggot-pie
puking	knotty-pated	malt-worm
puny	milk-livered	mammet
qualling	motley-minded	measle
rank	onion-eyed	minnow
reeky	plume-plucked	miscreant
roguish	pottle-deep	moldwarp

Adjective	Adjective	Noun
ruttish	pox-marked	mumble-news
saucy	reeling-ripe	nut-hook
spleeny	rough-hewn	pigeon-egg
spongy	rude-growing	pignut
surly	rump-fed	puttock
tottering	shard-borne	pumpion
unmuzzled	sheep-biting	ratsbane
vain	spur-galled	scut
venomed	swag-bellied	skainsmate
villainous	tardy-gaited	strumpet
warped	tickle-brained	varlot
wayward	toad-spotted	vassal
weedy	unchin-snouted	whey-face
yeasty	weather-bitten	wagtail

Prewriting/Writing Games

riting isn't just putting pen to paper. It's a process that starts with an idea and ends up as words on a page. At any point along the way, a child, especially one with learning difficulties, can get stuck.

If your child has trouble forming letters on paper, be his scribe until his coordination improves. After all, good writing is about good thinking and the clear expression of those thoughts; beautiful handwriting is a different skill. We encourage you to use these games to nurture your child's imagination and flexibility of mind.

Always Remember

- If you see that your child isn't enjoying the game, stop playing. Ask why she didn't like it. Get her ideas about how to make it better.

- At the end of every game, take stock together of the skills you worked on. Be lavish with praise for the things your child did well and be encouraging about the things she found difficult. Be as specific as possible.
- If your child is upset about something that's hard for her to do, remind her of the things she does well. Assure her of your faith in her ability to learn.

Hopping Sentences

Hopscotch all the way to good grammar.

Goals: Learn basic parts of speech and punctuation and compose simple sentences.
Materials: Chalk, paper, pen.
When/Where: On the sidewalk or at a playground.
The Game: Before you play, explain to your child, as simply as possible, about the parts of speech that make up a sentence—nouns, pronouns, verbs, adjectives, adverbs, conjunctions or connecting words, articles. (See "Parts of Speech" and "The Basic Sentence" in the Appendix.)

Draw or ask your child to draw the classic hopscotch pattern (see Figure 7.1) on the sidewalk or pavement. Just outside the hopscotch grid, draw three punctuation boxes: one with a period (.), one with a question mark (?), and one with an exclamation point (!).

Together, think up ten words—the list must include nouns or pronouns, at least one verb, a bunch of adjectives, connecting words, and articles. Remember, the most basic sentence contains at least one noun or pronoun as the subject and an

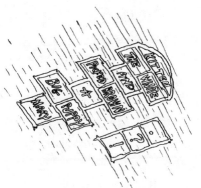

Figure 7.1 *Hopping Sentences*

appropriate verb. If you forget to include a noun or a verb on your word list, your child not might be able to play. That's a lesson in itself.

Write one word in each of the ten hopscotch boxes in random order. Each player must try to figure out a sentence using as many words/boxes as possible and then hop onto each word in sequence without stepping on the lines, just as in regular hopscotch. You can hop on a word more than once to build as long a sentence as you can, but the sentence must make sense. The final hop must be on an appropriate punctuation box. (All along, the nonhopping player should keep track of the boxes the hopper lands on.)

For example, your list might look like this:

Person, place, or thing (nouns or pronouns): *Mary* (or
  she), *puppy, kitten*
Action word (verb): *picked*
Describing word (adjective): *big, little, brown, white*
Connecting word (conjunction): *and*
Articles: *the* (or *a*)

With this list, the first player could hop *Mary picked the big brown puppy.* The second player could hop *Big Mary picked the little white kitten.* For the bonus point, you would need to include all the words: *Mary picked the big brown puppy and the little white kitten.* Other possibilities are *Little Mary picked the big white kitten and the little brown puppy* and *Little Mary picked the big white kitten and the big brown kitten and the little brown puppy and the little white puppy.*

As soon as your child completes a sentence, it's your turn. The more words the player can include in his hopping sentence, the more points he earns. He doesn't have to use all ten words in his sentence, but you can give him a bonus point if he is able to.

Keep taking turns until you've exhausted all possibilities. Then brainstorm another list and replace the old words on the hopscotch board with new ones.

Variations

■ Instead of making sentences, make questions (be sure you include question words, like *why, how,* and *when*). Or see who can hop the shortest sentence and still have it make sense—for example, *Go!* or *She laughed.*

■ Write or ask your child to write his sentence on paper when he's finished hopping it.

■ When you think your child has caught on to the components of a sentence, encourage him to make up the list of ten words on his own.

■ For a more sophisticated game, add adverbs, prepositions, and more connecting words or conjunctions.

Tips

- If your child feels discouraged by another player's facility—or your own—with composing sentences, play just for fun, not for points.
- Use a different chalk color for each part of speech.
- Number the boxes. In case the game moves along quickly, you can note the numbers of the boxes the hopper lands on in order and construct the sentence later.

Label the House

Race against the clock to stick up your home.

Goals: Practice writing, recognize words, and build and enrich vocabulary.

Materials: Post-it pads, pens or markers, stopwatch or egg timer.

When/Where: In the house, in a hotel, or in the home of a cooperative relative or friend.

The Game: Pick a room in the house, say, the kitchen. With your child, name ten things in the room: big things, like the refrigerator, countertop, oven or stove (show her the difference); and small things, like the cookie jar, salt and pepper shakers, etc. Make a list of the items. Ask your child to copy the name of each item onto its own Post-it. Lay the Post-its on a table and read each one together.

The object of the game is to see how many items in the room your child can correctly label in one minute. At the word

Go, she must pick up one Post-it, read it out loud, stick it onto the corresponding item, then come back for the next label, and so on until the time runs out.

Together, go around the room and see how many items were labeled correctly. Any incorrect label should be put in its proper place.

In round two, your child picks another room, say, her bedroom, and names ten items to be found, listed, and written on Post-its. Then it's your turn to see how many labels you can post in thirty seconds (use the timer or have your child count the seconds). You may be surprised by how difficult it is to properly label all the Beanie Babies on the bookshelf or each doll in the dollhouse from Barbie to the Power Puff Girls.

Variations

- Label things inside drawers or closets and on the refrigerator.
- Label items throughout the house. Depending on how big your home is, players may need to be quick readers and runners to beat the clock.
- For advanced play, write clues on the Post-its instead of names. Players must then figure out each clue and place the label on the correct item. If, for example, your Post-it reads, *It really heats up inside*, your child will have to label the oven, microwave, or dishwasher.
- Have your child time *you* as you write the labels.

Tips

- When writing labels with your child, don't worry if she copies an item incorrectly. When you review the words together, you can guide her to correct the spelling.

■ You can do all the reading and writing if necessary, but have your child repeat the words if you read them.

■ Have younger children focus on the first letter of the words when you read the labels together. Be sure to write in all capital letters to avoid confusion among the letters *b*, *d*, and *p*. Keep the words simple and try not to use the same initial letter for more than one item. For example, don't make a label for the chair and the couch when you first begin to play this game.

■ Leave the labels on their respective items for a day or so after you've finished playing. Your child can practice reading *lamp* the next time she turns it on.

Unfolding Poetry

Even kids who hate writing find there's no pressure and lots of surprises in this collaborative game.

Goals: Practice writing and sequencing and spark imagination.
Materials: A legal-size sheet of lined paper, different-colored pencils.
When/Where: Anywhere. This game works best with at least three people playing.
The Game: Each player picks a different-color pen or pencil. Player one writes a word or several words on the first line of the paper. The words can be on any subject. They can paint a

word picture (*Orange sun*) or suggest an action (*Emmett sings*). Imaginative writing is encouraged. The player then folds the top of the paper over so that his writing cannot be seen and passes the sheet to the next player.

Player two adds his own phrase—without knowing what player one has written! The idea is to keep this process going until the sheet is filled. Then unfold the paper and ask your child to read the results. What often emerges is the beginning of an intriguing poem. You might get something like this: "Emmett sings/I want to play/Sun and fun/Let's go.

Variations

- Cut up the different lines and rearrange them to make a different or more pleasing or sillier poem.
- Before you begin, discuss a topic to write about—for example, "a winter's day" or "a good friend."
- Write a story instead of a poem. In that case, each line must be a complete sentence. (See "The Basic Sentence" in the Appendix.)
- It's cool to create the poem on black paper using gel pens.
- Illustrate the poem or story when you're done.
- Collect the poems in a binder and compile an "Unfolded Poetry" series. When you have enough, organize a family "Poetry Slam"—a reading with music.

Tips

- If your child or any other young player has difficulty writing, team up with him and have him whisper a phrase for you to write.

■ If your child does the writing, tell him not to worry about spelling. You can correct misspelled words at the end of the game.

The Charlotte Game

The word-loving spider in Charlotte's Web *inspires a game that encourages writing and acquiring new words.*

Goal: Practice writing words and build vocabulary.
Materials: Post-its, pencil and paper, a children's dictionary.
When/Where: At home.
The Game: If you haven't yet read E. B. White's classic *Charlotte's Web* to your child, it's never too late to begin. This game replicates Charlotte the spider's instructions to Templeton the Rat in Chapter 18: to venture forth onto the county fairgrounds, hunt among the leftover food wrappers and discarded newspapers, and "Bring back a word!" that will save Wilbur the pig's life.

Here's our version of Charlotte's assignment: Check out the contents of your pantry or refrigerator and find a really good word on a package of food. Depending on your child's vocabulary, you might decide on a simple word, like *crunchy* from a cereal box, or go for a tougher word like *saturated* from the nutrition label on a tunafish can.

Print the word on a Post-it and give it to your child. Allow her enough time to (1) find one food product with the word on it, (2) figure out what the word means—from the context on the box, from the dictionary, or by asking someone—and (3) stick the Post-it on the refrigerator door. (On a typical cereal box, we recently located words such as *receive, enlarged, commitment, accelerator,* and *notorious*.)

Then it's her turn to post a word for *you* to find!

Variations

- If you want to link this game more explicitly to *Charlotte's Web*, draw (or ask your child to draw) a spiderweb on a colorful piece of paper, tape the drawing to the fridge, and post your word in the center of the web, as Charlotte did.

- Ask your child to help you write a sentence using the word. Then post the sentence on the refrigerator.

- Try a supermarket version of the game: Write the target word on an index card before you go shopping. As you cruise the aisles, see how many packages you both can find that contain the word. (This may make shopping with your child much more enjoyable!)

- If your child is a beginning reader, put four food products on the kitchen counter and ask her to search for a specific letter.

Tips

- Since this is a food-based game, you may want to provide an edible reward if your child completes the assignment.

- If your child struggles with writing, let her dictate words or sentences to you and then have her copy what you've written.

- If your child writes a sentence with a found word, make sure it is complete: *I ate my crunchy cereal* is complete; *Crunchy cereal* isn't. If your child is having trouble composing a complete sentence, gently help her out. (See "The Basic Sentence" in the Appendix.)

■ Encourage your child to keep a list of the new words she is learning. Even better, record the new words in a "personal dictionary"—like a notebook or in a date book with lots of blank pages.

■ Try to use the web-words in your daily conversation. Comment on how *crunchy* crackers are or how well the rain *saturated* the soil in the garden.

Squeaky-Clean Tales

A sudsy game that nurtures the imagination and the art of storytelling.

Goal: Learn how the five *W*s build a story.

When/Where: The bathtub at bathtime.

Materials: Foam soap or shaving cream, bath paints or soap crayons, a tiled wall or a mirror, paper, index cards, pencils or markers.

The Game: At bath time, invite your child to help you create a story while she's splashing in the tub. Explain that stories usually contain the five *W*s: who, when, where, what, and why.

Have your child write five *W*s on the tiled wall with the foam soap or shaving cream. The object of the game is to make up a story by starting with one *W* and working your way through the remaining four—in any order.

For example, start by asking your child to tell you *who* the story is about (a made-up character? someone she knows? a favorite fairy-tale character or cartoon hero?), *when* the story takes place (today? in the future? in the past?), and *where* the story begins (in your town? in a thick forest? in outer space?). Next, decide *what* the character does first and *why* (a prince sets off into the forest on a quest to find a unicorn; a young girl builds a rocket to go to Mars to prevent a powerful meteor from hitting the earth). Keep track of your child's answers—you may want to take notes.

Now it's time to tell the story. *You* begin the tale, using the elements your child imagined. Encourage her to help you flesh out the story with vivid details or twists in the plot. Prompt by using one of the five *Ws*: *Who* did the prince meet in the forest? (A dragon.) *What* was he doing and *why*? (Cooking an egg for dinner with his fiery breath.) Chances are your child will end up creating most of the story herself by adding one detail at a time—with your guidance.

Variations

- Next time you play, *you* think up the *Ws* and ask your child to make up a story.
- Invite your child to use crayon soap to draw illustrations or a map on the wall relating to the story.
- Think about a favorite tale, like "Sleeping Beauty," and see how many of the five *Ws* you can find in it.
- Create a Squeaky-Clean *series* by using the same characters but adding more *Ws* for variety each time your child takes a bath.
- Make a book of the stories you create and leave them in the bathroom for future reading.

Tips

- Each time you play, write the five *Ws* as a reminder on the bathroom tiles with soap or shaving cream.

You can stick to the same characters if you like, but at least one of the other *W*s has to change.

■ If your child is reluctant to get started, you can provide the details and start things off. Then pretend to get stuck and ask your child for help.

Recycled Stories

Can you turn an old story into a new one?

Goals: Practice writing, sequencing, and storytelling and build vocabulary.

Materials: Old, worn-out, or damaged children's books that have been outgrown; old magazines or comic books; scissors; two or three sheets of blank paper; index cards; and glue.

When/Where: Best played at home—perhaps on a long, rainy afternoon.

The Game: With your child, cut sentences out of two or three damaged or worn books or magazines. Take turns rearranging them to make a new story. If he needs extra words to complete a story or a thought, he can write them on an index card.

Once the sentences have been rearranged to make up the new tale, paste them in order onto the blank sheets of paper to make a book. Don't forget to "write" a cover page with a title and the name of the author—your child.

Variations

■ If your child is a beginning reader, make an alphabet book. Cut out words that begin with each letter of the alphabet. Arrange them in order and illustrate the pages.

- Use your sentences to compose a poem. Or cut up a real poem and make a new one.
- Cut out an illustration and write a tale with a new twist—perhaps Sleeping Beauty is only pretending to be under a spell.

Tips

- Allow plenty of time for this game: it will take you and your child a while to find sentences in the books and then to cut and paste them onto paper.
- Keep adding to the book—write an ending or a sequel the usual way—with pencil and paper!
- Check out garage sales in your neighborhood or library book sales—they're a great source for cheap, recyclable children's books.

Vowel Stories

The short and long of writing with vowels.

Goals: Recognize vowels through writing, build vocabulary, practice sequencing and expressive language.

When/Where: Anytime, anywhere.

Materials: This game works best if you have an erasable surface to write on so you can add or change words easily. But pencil and paper will do fine.

The Game: The object of this game is to write a story with your child with one condition: all sentences must include at least one word that has a particular vowel sound, but the more, the better.

Pick a vowel to work on. (See "Vowels for Vowel Games" in the Appendix.) Start with a short vowel sound, because most of the words beginning readers learn first have short vowels in them (like *cat*, *bit*, *nut*). If your child gets frustrated, switch to long vowels.

To get your child into the swing of it, write a possible title for the story that includes the sound you selected. Have her tell the story to you as you write. Encourage her to stretch her imagination. Help her develop the story by offering a funny or interesting word that features the target sound, but make sure she feels she's in control.

Here's one Isaac "wrote" focusing on the short /ĭ/:

The W*i*tch with the Terr*i*ble *I*tch

Once upon a time, a nasty old *witch* had a *terrible itch*. She tried to *lick it*, but the nasty old *witch* could not get *rid* of that *itch*. She *bit* the *itch* and *kicked* the *itch*, but *it didn't* work. She even tried to *dig* a hole and get *in it*, but the *itch* was too *big*. So she *hid it*. *It* got so bad *it* made her *sick*. One day, someone gave her a *fig*. That *did it*! When she *bit* that *fig*, the *itch* was gone. And the *witch did* a *jig* to rejoice.

When you've completed the story, ask your child to find all the words that include the sound you're working on and underline them. Then have him read the story out loud, or you can read it for him.

Afterward, make changes and adjustments. Explain that writers write and then rewrite until the story sounds just right.

For example, you could add even more short /ĭ/ sounds to this story by changing *nasty* to *wicked, the itch was gone* to *she ditched the itch* or *the itch desisted* and *rejoice* to *in jubilation.*

Variations

- You can move away from vowel sounds and pick any phonics or spelling pattern your child needs work on—such as blends or word families. (See "Consonant Blends" and "Word Families" in the Appendix.)
- Write a story using letters your child might get confused, like *b* and *d* or *p* and *q*. (See "Confusable Words and Letters" in the Appendix.)
- Keep the stories together and make a book out of them. If your child likes to draw, he can illustrate each story.
- In the car, you can make up vowel stories without writing them down.

Tips

- For children who have trouble getting started, prompt with a classic story opening, like "Once upon a time" or "In a land far, far away," or suggest an opening sentence such as *There once was an elegant elephant who enjoyed exceptional eggs.* But you can start with anything. Sometimes it's fun to begin with an exclamation like "BANG!" or "OOPS!" And then explain what just happened.
- Make sure your child knows the meaning of any difficult words that you put in the story.

Word by Word

The longer the sentence, the more the pennies add up.

Goals: Practice writing, expanding ideas, and sequencing.
Materials: Lined paper, pencils, a hundred pennies.
When/Where: Anytime, anywhere.
The Game: In this game, a team of players must build a sentence word by word that's as long as possible. An adult should monitor the sentence as it grows to make sure it makes sense. (See "The Basic Sentence" in the Appendix.)

The game is limited to three rounds. In round one, the first player (preferably an adult) writes one word on the first line of the paper and reads it aloud. On line two, player two reads and rewrites the first word, says and then writes a second word that can logically follow. Player three, on line three, reads and rewrites the first two words and adds a third. And so it goes until the team decides to end the sentence, punctuating only at the end.

If your child can read, have him read the final sentence out loud. Then the team totals the number of words in the final sentence and awards itself a penny for each word.

For example, your paper might look something like this in the beginning:

Player one: *One*
Player two: *One day*
Player three: *One day we*
Player four: *One day we went.* . . .

. . . and the result could be a lovely run-on sentence like this: "One day we went to the park and played on the jungle gym and afterward we went to eat ice cream in a little shop around the corner that has a green awning and an owner with a funny mustache that droops over his chin."

Clearly, this sentence could be terminated at several points along the way (after *park* or *played* or *gym* or *eat* or *cream* or *shop* or *corner* or *awning* or *mustache*). But remember: the longer the sentence, the more pennies the team racks up—so it's in the team's interest to keep the sentence moving along.

In rounds two and three, players launch a new sentence with the goal of making it even longer than the previous one. The object is to rack up a total of a hundred words (and therefore a hundred pennies).

Variations

- Start playing with declarative sentences (sentences that state something and require periods at the end), then vary with questions (sentences that begin with question words such as *How many* or *Why* or *Who* and that require question marks at the end).

- Up the ante: build a story. In each round, require that the new sentence extend the subject of the previous one. (So our example might be followed by a new sentence that would elaborate on what happened next—*after* the trip to the ice cream parlor. You could start with *When we finished our ice cream . . .*).

- To practice editing and revising, take your longest sentence and rewrite it, dividing it into short, simple sentences.

■ Illustrate your sentences or your story at the end of the game.

■ If you prefer, tape long strips of brown wrapping paper to a wall and write the words in large letters.

Tips

■ As a sentence expands, encourage your child to read the accumulated words fluently, with appropriate expression.

■ Don't interrupt if your child writes a word incorrectly. Rather, when it's your turn to add a word, rewrite the misspelled word correctly.

aption It

A picture's worth a thousand words, but you have to write only a few.

Goals: Practice writing, interpret pictures, and understand point of view.

Materials: Family photos (or, second best, photos from a magazine or newspaper), paper, pencils, a good imagination.

When/Where: Anytime, anywhere you have access to pictures and writing materials. This game works best with three or more players.

The Game: You know how much fun it is to pull out the old family photo album or look at snapshots from your most recent vacation. Now you can reminisce while strengthening visual comprehension and writing skills.

Take five to ten family photos or cut out intriguing pictures from a magazine or newspaper. Spread them out face up on a table.

Each player selects (to herself) one photo on the table. On a piece of paper, players write a caption for the photo they've chosen secretly. The caption can be a comment on what's going on in the picture or a made-up quote inspired by one of the subjects.

Players cannot simply describe a picture or state where it was taken. Their caption must add a new element to the snapshot. For example, Isaac chose a picture of himself floating in a swimming pool. He could have written many things, such as "Now all I need is a cool glass of lemonade." His caption was "Aaaah."

When everyone has finished writing, go around the table in order from youngest to oldest and begin reading each of the captions out loud. If your child cannot write on her own, she can say her caption and then have a grown-up write it down for her.

The other players try to identify the picture that matches the caption. If they are successful, the writer places her caption next to the photo. However, if no one can make a match, the writer places her caption on the picture, reads it again, and explains why she wrote that particular one.

This may spark a discussion about how one interprets a photograph. If more than one player writes a caption for the same photo, that's fine.

Once a photo has been captioned, it is taken off the table. Continue playing until all the pictures have been captioned. If you want, paste the captions in your photo album.

Variations

- Combine two or more of the pictures and write captions that tell a story.
- Have each player write a caption for the same photo. Then compare the different interpretations of the same picture.
- Make this a vocabulary game by writing a list of action words (*fishing, screaming, frolicking*) and see if you can find photos to match.
- Use photos of two or more people and write words they might say to each other. You could develop this variation into a full-fledged play or photo novella, with lots of dialogue.

Tips

- For children who struggle with writing, you can write their caption and then have them copy it.
- Unless your child asks for help, don't worry about spelling mistakes. You can correct them when the round is over.

Writing for Ransom

A cut-and-paste extortion game.

Goals: Skim for words, construct full sentences, and compose instructions.

Materials: Old newspapers or magazines or worn-out children's books; scissors; a sheet of paper; glue; one of your favorite things; a fun, edible reward.

When/Where: Best played at home.

The Game: Ask your child if she knows what a ransom note is. If she doesn't, explain: when a thief steals something valuable, she may decide to return it to the owner for ransom, or a certain sum of money. To avoid being caught, she makes up a ransom note, disguising her handwriting by cutting and pasting words from magazines.

Pick one of your favorite things: a photograph, an old toy, or a book. Whatever you choose, give it to your child, close your eyes, and tell her to hide it somewhere in the house.

Her next task is to compose a short ransom note, cutting letters and words from the printed material and pasting them onto the sheet of paper. This is best done together since it may take a while to find, cut, and paste all the text you need to make the note.

The ransom note should specify what the stolen object is ("I have your photograph!") and what you must pay in ransom ("If you want it back, pay me one dish of ice cream!"). Once your child has completed the note, you must hand over the edible reward in exchange for the stolen object!

As your child gets the hang of this game, have her add details such as *Bring the ransom to the kitchen. Come alone!* or *Make sure there are two full scoops. And extra sprinkles!* Take turns being ransomer and ransomee.

Variations

- Instead of composing a ransom note, ask your child to cut and paste clues to where she has hidden the object. For example: *It's where we keep the dirty clothes!*
- Use this game to practice writing directions. For example, have your child indicate exactly where you

must go to find the object: *Walk into the kitchen, turn to face the wall with the clock, take two steps toward the cabinet, open the bottom drawer* . . . and so on.

Tips

- Collect materials with big print—such as advertisements or headlines.
- If your child has difficulty using scissors, cut out the words she chooses. But let her choose! You're there to help, not to impose your ideas.
- If your child misreads a word—say she cuts out *you* instead of *your*—help her find the correct word in a magazine.
- As your child gets better at the game, have her check to make sure the word is clear and that she's written complete sentences. Don't forget punctuation— periods or question marks or exclamation points. (See "The Basic Sentence" in the Appendix.)
- Every time you play, up the ante: encourage your child to write a longer note—first one sentence, then two, then three . . .
- If your child needs help organizing her thoughts, have her answer these questions: What's been taken? What is the ransom you demand? When and where will the kidnapped object be returned?

8

Miscellaneous Games

ast but not least, here's a grab bag of games that strengthen skills you may not associate with learning to read and write: skills like physical coordination, organizing ideas into categories, thinking of alternative ways to solve problems, and much more.

As a bonus, helping children develop these skills enhances their ability to confront the challenges of life that aren't in print.

Always Remember

- If you see that your child isn't enjoying the game, stop playing. Ask why she didn't like it. Get her ideas about how to make it better.
- At the end of every game, take stock together of the skills you worked on. Be lavish with praise for the

things your child did well and be encouraging about the things she found difficult. Be as specific as possible.

■ If your child is upset about something that's hard for her to do, remind her of the things she does well. Assure her of your faith in her ability to learn.

What If

There's always more than one way to solve a problem.

Goals: Solve problems by coming up with alternative strategies, practice critical thinking, and build imagination.

Materials: Nothing but a brain.

When/Where: A good game for when you're on the road in a car, train, or bus. Any number of people can play.

The Game: Player one presents a problem or a situation of any kind: social, academic, or physical. Player two must come up with three possible solutions or strategies to solve the problem or respond to the situation, as follows:

> The first solution has to be one the player can accomplish on his own.
> The second solution should involve someone who can help him.
> The third solution should be whimsical or magical.

For example, player one could present the following problem: "You are in the cafeteria, and a friend of yours says that if you don't share your dessert, he won't be your friend anymore. What can you do?"

Possible solutions: (1) Tell the person that a real friend wouldn't do that. (2) Ask another kid in school to eat lunch with you. (3) Create a giant bubble, blow it around the mean kid, and send him into the sky.

Then player two creates a situation for player one to tackle, such as "What if you were asked to test sixty new video games—but you had only one hour to do it? If you complete the test, you can keep them all. If you don't finish, you get nothing. How can you make sure that all of the games get tested?"

Possible answers: (1) Working alone, you might test each game for only one minute. (2) Invite fifty-nine friends to each test one game with you. (3) Put on your winged shoes and speed through the games.

Variations

- Pose a real-life problem or situation that your child is facing. For example, "Imagine you are going to a new school and you feel nervous. How would you deal with the situation?" Possible solutions: (1) "I could visit the school and check it out in advance." (2) "I could go the office and ask the secretary if there's anybody from my neighborhood or my old school who will be in my class." (3) "I would invent this machine. It would spray kids with stuff that would make them like me."
- Play the game using only wacky solutions or ones that involve asking someone for help.

Tips

- Don't force your child to deal with a real problem she may be having if she's not able to handle it. The point of the game is to learn to think about options in playful ways.
- Mix up serious problems with more lighthearted dilemmas or situations.

Total Recall

A fun workout for your body and your memory.

Goals: Follow and issue multistep instructions and help build coordination.

Materials: Nothing but bodies, brains, and whatever you see around you.

When/Where: Anyplace, anytime. Adjust the tasks to the physical restraints of your location.

The Game: Tell your child to do something physical. Start with something simple, such as "Touch your head." Then add another task: "Touch your head and run to the window," and so on.

Continue with instructions, repeating them in order before adding a new one. Play until your child completes a sequence of five or six tasks—and then it's your turn to take orders.

As you progress in the game, add more commands—and make them more complex and/or specific: "Clap your hands, run very fast to the tree, count to ten by twos, untie your shoes, then tie them again, run back."

Variations

- If your child has difficulty writing, manipulating small objects, and using scissors, or trouble with coordination, balance, hopping, etc. , you can incorporate activities to help strengthen these motor skills: "Touch your left shoulder with your right hand, pick up a pen, draw a picture of a flower," and so forth.

- You can sneak in a review of phonics skills (see "Simple Basic Phonics" in the Appendix): "Pick up the pen, turn around, jump three times, write the letter that makes the /t/ sound—and eat a cookie."

- Focus on direction words, like *under* or *underneath*, *below, above, on top of, next to, to the right, to the left, beside*: "Turn to the right and crawl under the table, come out, turn to the left, pick up the ball, put it on top of the table with your right hand," and so on.

- You can play this game in slow motion or at super speed.

- If you wish, at the end of each series of actions, the child can yell "Total recall!" If he forgets this final action, he has to start over.

Tips

- Start with a short list of tasks (three to five) as your goal for the first set. You want to make sure your child succeeds at first before pushing him to do more tasks in a set. Gradually increase as your child's memory improves.

- Vary the tasks, alternating things your child does easily with more challenging ones.

Category Pitch

Good pitchers can toss the same object into different categories.

Goals: Classify objects, notice details, and help strengthen memory.

When/Where: At home, in the park, at the beach—anytime.

Materials: Things to throw, like pennies, shells, sticks, small stones; someplace to toss them around in—like a yard, the basement, or even the living room (if you toss light objects such as rolled-up socks).

The Game: Begin by explaining what categories are: groups of things that have something in common. The category *animals* includes all living creatures like lions, tigers, sharks, parrots, butterflies, and humans. However, these creatures have attributes that qualify them to fit into other categories. Sharks, for example, can also be considered fish or predators; parrots can be categorized, among other things, as birds or talking animals. Lions can be categorized as mammals, large cats, four-legged beasts, and meat-eaters or carnivores.

Select an object from your house for your child to categorize: a toy, a picture, or something in the room. Then tell him to pick up the item to be tossed—the stick or penny or pebble—and throw it as far as he can. *At the same time*, he must name a category to which the object you've named belongs. The point of the game is to see how many categories he can think up while he's strengthening his pitching arm.

For example, suppose you picked his favorite Hot Wheels car. In what categories could he put it? Toys? Automobiles? Objects with wheels? Small objects? Plastic objects? Shiny objects? (Or, if he wants to be whimsical: things my mom will let me buy that cost about a dollar?)

When your child has run out of categories, you may count up the pennies or sticks he's thrown and jot the number on a scorecard. Then your child selects an object for you to categorize as you throw.

Variations

- Instead of throwing free-style, your child can aim for a tree or a box or even a circle on the ground.
- Instead of selecting an object that can be seen, name one your child must visualize.
- Ask your child to select his own object to classify. Start with a category—say, amphibians—and ask your child to think of as many as he can.

Tips

- If your child has difficulty thinking of categories, let him do the pitching while you do the classifying. Eventually he'll get the idea.
- If he names an incorrect category, gently correct him.

Dom-in-o, Dom-in-oes

Stack up the syllables as you play an old favorite.

Goals: Develop awareness of syllabication and help build vocabulary.
Materials: A standard box of dominoes (with twenty-eight tiles) with rules, a children's dictionary.
When/Where: Anywhere, anytime.

The Game: Does your child know what a syllable is? If not, explain that it's a building block of a word. Some words have only one syllable, while others have two or more.

A simple way to demonstrate this idea is by clapping in time to the syllables. Start with a single-syllable name, like *Ann* or *Joe*. As you say the name, clap once. Then clap out your names. If your name is *Es-mer-el-da*, you will clap four times for four syllables. Now get out the domino box. Spread all twenty-eight tiles face down on a tabletop and shuffle them. Take turns picking seven dominoes from the set and arranging them so that the other player can't see the dots. (If there are three or four players, pick only five dominoes each.)

The first player lays down one domino. The second player has to match one of the two numbers on the first domino by laying her tile down matching end to matching end. (See Figure 8.1.) As she lays the tile, she must also say a word with the same number of syllables as the dots on the matching end. If she can't make a match, she must keep picking tiles from the extra pile until she can find a tile with matching dots. A blank tile is "wild": any number of syllables can be declared.

If your child can't come up with an appropriate word, give her clues. (For a two-syllable word, you might prompt with "Something you write with that doesn't have ink"—for *pen-cil* or *cray-on*.) The first person to get rid of all her dominoes wins.

Possible words are *cat*, *rug*, or *plate* for one dot; *hap-py* or *danc-ing* for two dots; *pic-nick-ing* for three, and so on all the way up to six. You can think of more than one word for your syllable match: for example, *hap-py dog* for three dots, *Mon-day af-ter-noon* for five, or *mac-a-ron-i and cheese* for six.

Keep a running list of the words you come up with as you play. Do not repeat words. At the end of the game you can read

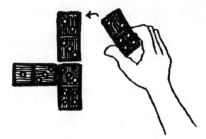

Figure 8.1 *Dom-in-o, Dom-in-oes*

the words back and say how many "dots" or syllables are in each word.

Variations

- Before you play, write words of varying syllables on index cards for reference.
- Up the ante by requiring each player to think up two words per tile—matching the dots on either end.
- To make things even harder and expand awareness of items in a group, restrict the words to a certain category. For instance, if you think of words only for animals, you might say *horse* for one dot; *hip-po* for two; *ant-eat-er* for three, *cat-er-pil-lar* for four; *Ty-ran-no-sau-rus* for five; and *Ty-ran-no-sau-rus Rex* for six.

Tips

- Encourage your child to look around the room for clues to words.
- If your child gets really stuck, use a children's dictionary to hunt for multisyllabic words. Point out how the dictionary breaks up words with dots in between the syllables.

■ If your child can write, have her keep the list of words—but don't let her struggle with spelling. Help her out if she's having trouble!

Memory Café

Ordering dinner is a fun way to keep your child's memory in order.

Goals: Build memory, practice sequencing, master details, and take notes.

When/Where: This is a good rainy-day home game. It works best with three or more players.

Materials: Paper and pencils or markers; a small notebook or pad adds a sense of realism to the game.

The Game: Have your child create a menu that contains at least twenty items. (You can use a take-out menu as a reference if you need to.) Make sure he includes different categories of food: appetizers, main dishes, side dishes, desserts, beverages. If he has trouble writing, you can write the food choices as he names them. He can also decorate the menu after you've written all the items down.

Let your child take the first turn playing waiter. Pass the menu around and let each player pick one item as the waiter writes it down. If your child has trouble writing, he can write a letter or symbol that represents the food being ordered.

After all players have placed their orders, the waiter must go around the table and repeat each order correctly without looking at his notes. If the waiter remembers every order correctly, pass the menu again, have the guests pick two items, and repeat. Keep adding items to the orders until the waiter forgets an item, at which point someone else takes a turn. (Each guest must remember his or her order—or one adult can keep notes.)

Variations

■ To make the game more challenging, complicate the orders. Start with "Spaghetti with sauce on the side" or "Tea with a big slice of lemon" and gradually work up to "I would like my juice first, but it should be in a colorful glass, and I want my spaghetti on the upper-left-hand corner of my plate, and my peas should be in the lower right corner."

■ Guests can place a "scrambled order"—that is, dessert first, appetizer in the middle, and so forth—which the waiter has to unscramble and restate in the sequence it will be served.

■ If you're dining out, ask your child to memorize everybody's order and then restate it to the server.

■ For a real challenge, use an actual take-out menu with lots of different categories and types of food.

■ Use a mail-order catalog, change the waiter into a salesperson, and have the players memorize the items they plan to buy.

Tips

■ Keep the game simple at first, until your child gets the hang of it. Make it more challenging bit by bit— but not so difficult that he gets frustrated.

■ As the game gets more complicated, tell your child he can rely on his memory or use his notes for quick reference.

Keyboard Kinetics

Let your fingers do the walking and see what words are at the end of the road.

Goals: Practice using a computer keyboard, listening, finding letters and words in a word search puzzle, and spelling.

Materials: Computer word-processing program, paper to print on, pens or pencils.

When/Where: Anyplace you have access to a computer. The game works best with two players.

The Game: For children who struggle with the mechanics of writing, the computer can be an invaluable tool to express ideas on paper. This game will help your child practice using a keyboard while creating a word-search puzzle for you to play together.

Open a word-processing program on the computer. Hit the Caps Lock key and choose a large font size for easy reading. Warm up by exploring the keyboard together, taking turns reading the letters out loud, tapping the keys, and noting the location (and function) of the space bar and enter key.

Next, ask your child to place the fingers of her left hand, from the pinky to the index finger, on the keys *A-S-D-F*. Then ask her to place her right hand, from the index finger to the pinky, on the keys *J-K-L-;*. This is the *home* position for typing. Notice that on a computer the *F* and *J* keys have "bumps" on them to help you place your index fingers on the correct keys without looking.

When your child is in position at the keyboard, begin the game by calling out ten letters, one letter at a time. They can be random or repetitive, but make sure you have a good mix of vowels and consonants. (See "Simple Basic Phonics" in the Appendix.) As your child hears a letter, she must find and tap the corresponding key on the keypad and then hit the space bar two times. She may look at the keys but should make an attempt to use all eight fingers to type the letters (the two thumbs are used to tap the spacebar). After typing ten letters, have your child hit the enter key two times.

Switch places so you type as your child calls out ten letters. Remind her to include vowels. Ask her to look over your shoulder as you type—to get more practice spotting and reading letters.

After you have completed five rows of ten letters each, print the page. What you've created is your own word-search puzzle. Working as a team, try to find as many words as possible and then circle the words. To make a word, letters must be next to each other horizontally, vertically, or on a diagonal. (See Figure 8.2.) If you have trouble finding words, next time make sure you have a better mix of vowels and consonants.

Variations

■ As your child becomes more familiar with the keyboard, urge her to type without looking at it.

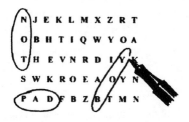

Figure 8.2 Keyboard Kinetics

- Mix uppercase with lowercase letters for more of a typing challenge.
- A typewriter will do if you don't have a computer.

Tips

- Speed is not important in this game. If your child has trouble finding the letters, help her. With practice she will improve her typing speed—and you can call out letters faster.
- For writing practice, have your child make a list of the words you find in the word-search puzzle. And if you wish, write a story using them.
- As you type, your child may not be able to resist calling out letters that spell his name or that make a sentence, such as "M-I-C-H-A-E-L I-S C-O-O-L." That's fine as it will give him spelling practice and guarantee at least three words will be found. Just make sure he dictates random letters as well.

From Here to There

Wordplay's version of Hangman.

Goals: Correct spelling and build vocabulary.
Materials: Paper, a pencil or a pen, an alphabet list, a children's dictionary.
When/Where: Anywhere, anytime.
The Game: In the classic game of Hangman, one player thinks of a word and writes a number of short blank lines that equal the number of letters in the word (say, if the word is

jump, there would be four blank lines _ _ _ _). The other players have to fill in the blanks with the vowels and consonants that make up the word. (See "Simple Basic Phonics" in the Appendix.) Each wrong letter guess allows player one to draw one of six body parts of the "hanged man"—first his torso, then two arms and two legs, and finally his head inside a noose. After all six parts of the hanged man have been drawn, the players get one final chance to guess the word. If they fail, the "hanged man" is history.

In this version of Hangman, the first player thinks of two letters—a beginning letter and an ending letter. The goal for the other players is to think of as many words as they can that share the same start and finish. (Player one must secretly write down at least two words that fit the bill.)

For example, player one (preferably an adult) thinks of two words that begin with *s* and end with *e*—in this case *snake* and *slice*. She then writes *s* on the *left* edge of a piece of paper and *e* on the *right* edge. In this game there are no blank lines since her opponents can come up with suitable words of any length (from *Sue* to *shave*—to *suitable*, for that matter).

The players take turns thinking of letters (refer to the alphabet list if need be) that take us from here—*s*—to there—*e*. Keep the game going until, collectively, a designated writer (probably you) has compiled a list of words that go from here to there in different ways. Players get a point for every correct word completed and an extra two points for every word they guess that player one had in mind. Then the next player takes a turn writing down two secret words that share a beginning and ending and writing down their first and last letters to show the others. Everyone should use a dictionary or ask someone to check spellings of secret words.

If you wish, follow the Hangman rules to increase the level of "danger": for each incorrect word proposed (say someone guesses *sneak* or *scream* for the S—E word), the first player can add a body part to the Hangman drawing until the full man has been hanged.

Variations

- Restrict the words to nouns (*shack, steak, shark*), verbs (*smack, seek, smirk*), or adjectives (*sick, slack, slick*). (See "Parts of Speech" in the Appendix.)
- Instead of beginning and ending letters, use words from your child's spelling list.

Tips

- If a mystery word begins with *q*, add *u*—these letters are always together.
- If your child gets really stuck, give clues to words that you've chosen: for example, for *snake*, say "It's something that looks like its first letter."
- Play in teams if the game is too difficult for your child to make guesses on his own.

Bang the Word Slowly

Get loud, get savvy about syllables.

Goals: Practice syllabication and build vocabulary.

Materials: Alphabet letters in a bag or hat; something to bang with—like sticks or chopsticks; something to bang on—like pots, pans, rocks, or drums.

When/Where: Anytime, anyplace you can be loud.

The Game: If your child does not know what a syllable is, explain by showing her how to count the beats in a person's name as you clap your hands or beat your drum. So if your name is *Sue*, you would clap your hands or beat the drum once. If your child's name is *Emily*, she would clap or beat *Em-i-ly* (three times).

Put the alphabet letters in the bag or hat. Player one closes her eyes and pulls out a letter. She shows the letter to the other players, then thinks of a one-syllable or one-beat word beginning with that letter. As she says the word, she claps out (or drums out) the beat. Using the same letter, player two says and claps or bangs a two-syllable word that begins with the letter. So it goes until players run out of ideas for new words.

For example, the letter *A* might prompt players to bang out (1) *ant*, (2) *ap-ple*, (3) *an-i-mal*, (4) *an-i-ma-tion*, (5) *ar-gu-men-ta-tive*, and so on, all the way up (if possible) to *an-ti-dis-es-tab-lish-men-tar-i-an-is-m* for a whopping twelve beats! Then it's player two's turn to pull a letter out of the hat.

Variations

- Try to make sentences using the words you've banged out.
- Play this as a rhyming game. If player one picks an *r* and says "rug," player two might come up with *chug* or *pug* or *hug*. Then pull two letters out of the bag and try to rhyme them together—say, *f* and *s*, which might yield *fly* and *sky*.
- Come up with rhyming words with double syllables— like *fly-by* and *sky-high*—or with different numbers of syllables, like *nation* and *information* or *snow* and *tiptoe*.

Tips

- If your child can't think of multisyllabic words, give her hints. Eventually she'll get the idea. For example, if she draws a *c* and needs to come up with a three-syllable word, you might suggest "a little yellow bird that sings."
- Start off with one- and two-syllable words and gradually increase the number of syllables required.
- When it's your turn, try to think of colorful or exotic words so you can expand your child's vocabulary.

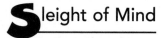leight of Mind

How to build a stronger memory with a little magic.

Goals: Build memory.

Materials: Pencil, paper.

When/Where: Anywhere, anytime. A great party trick.

The Game: For centuries magicians have performed feats of memory that have amazed audiences everywhere. Here's one of the secrets of their trade—a mental trick that prompts children to strengthen their memories by making associations among numbers, words, and images. Once your child has learned it, he will surely astound his own audiences of family and friends.

Help your child copy out and memorize the following list of numbers and words (it should be easy because everything rhymes):

One—sun
Two—shoe
Three—tree
Four—door

Five—beehive
Six—sticks
Seven—heaven
Eight—gate
Nine—vine
Ten—pen

Your child may need to practice reciting the list a few times to get it down pat. When he's feeling confident, call all the numbers out of order and see if he can name the rhyming objects.

Next, make a list of ten things, assigning each a number: for example, one—book; two—turtle; three—doorknob; four—horse; five—chair; six—television; seven—peanut butter sandwich; eight—bicycle; nine—cranberry juice; ten—reindeer.

Tell your child you're going to call out your list in order, pausing for a few seconds between objects. In that short time your child should make a mental picture of the word you call out, interacting with the appropriate number-object pair he's memorized. The more outrageous the mental picture, the more easily your child will be able to recall the object.

For example, when you call out item one, "book," your child might take a mental picture of the sun melting his favorite book. When you call out item three, "turtle," your child might visualize a turtle climbing a tree. And so on. The premise here is that when you make mental associations between things, you can remember them better.

Once you've finished reading your list out loud, start calling out numbers in any order. This is the amazing part: your child should be able to recall most—if not all—of the things on your list simply by hearing the number.

Practice this a bunch of times using different lists each time. When your child is ready, invite friends and family to make their own lists of objects to test his magical powers of recall.

Variations

- When you first call out your list of ten objects, name them in random order and then have your child say them back from one to ten or backward, from ten to one.
- Have your child recall objects in random order.
- Have your child test you by writing and calling out his list for you to remember.

Tips

- When your child is making a mental picture of the object on your list, prompt him to do so quickly. Don't let him take a long time to do this. The idea is to get a quick "snapshot" and then move on.
- Remember, the more active the mental image, the easier it will be to recall the item on your list. For example, rather than simply shining on a book, the sun should melt a book into a *boiling* puddle.

Pillow Jumps

Jump-start your child's memory and coordination.

Goals: Distinguish between left and right and build coordination and memory.

Materials: A large bed (preferably a queen or king size), some pillows.

When/Where: Anytime, anyplace you have a bed and pillows or open space.

The Game: This game originated in the bedroom using pillows and a large bed. If you don't have room to run in your bedroom, see the variations for how to adapt this game for the outdoors.

For Practice with Left and Right

First, ask your child to raise his left hand, then his right hand, to lift his left leg, then his right leg. If he is unsure, stand beside him facing in the same direction and have him follow you as you demonstrate left and right.

Next, position yourself at the end or on the side of the bed. Hold up a pillow above and over the bed. In this game your child will be running, jumping up, and landing on the bed, so make sure there is enough room for him to land safely.

Ask your child to stand in a starting position a few feet from the bed, enough so he can get a running start. Instruct him to run toward the bed, jump up, and hit the pillow with his left hand, shouting "left" as loud as he can.

If he used the wrong hand in the first instruction, remind him which is his left hand, then have him try again. Don't add a new step until he has mastered the current one. As long as your child gets to run and jump, it's unlikely he'll protest having to repeat an instruction. Keep it light and fun.

You may have to give instructions for one step at a time to reinforce which is left and which is right. If he does the sequence correctly, send him back to the starting position and add a second instruction: "Run and hit the pillow with your left hand, shouting 'left,' then hit it with your right hand, shouting 'right.'" You can eliminate the shouting as the sequences get more involved.

Continue adding steps until he has mastered five in a row. For example: (1) hit pillow with your left hand; (2) hit pillow with left, then right hand; (3) hit pillow with left, then right hand and roll; (4) hit the pillow with left, then right hand, roll, and hop back to the start on your left leg; (5) hit the pillow with left, then right hand, roll, hop back to start on left leg, and then kick right leg.

Once your child has successfully completed five steps, you take a turn (if he'll let you) and jump as he gives orders. Or begin again with a new set of instructions for your child.

For Coordination Practice

The object here is to practice grabbing a moving target or jumping through a homemade "hoop." Forget left and right this time. From your spot beside the bed, extend your arm and move the pillow up and down above and over the bed. Tell your child to run and grab the pillow before diving onto the bed. Once he can coordinate his movement to grab the pillow as you move it up and down, swing the pillow from side to side over the bed and have him grab it before he lands.

For a different challenge, get a second pillow and move both pillows up and down toward each other, like a jaw opening and closing. Tell your child to jump through the hole before the jaws close on him.

At the next level, combine the left-right game with the coordination game to hit a moving pillow. For example, have him grab the moving pillow with his left hand, then hop back to the starting line on his right foot.

Variations

- For a faster pace on the left-right game, wait until your child has run almost to the bed before you call out "left hand" or "right hand." This will give him less time to think and will help his understanding of left and right become automatic.
- Have your child hold another pillow while he runs. Before he jumps to hit your pillow, he must throw his pillow to you, not up in the air.
- Let your child jump on the bed while you swing a pillow just under his legs so he has to jump over it or just over his head so he has to duck under it. Be unpredictable in your choices to work his reflexes.
- Let your child tell you what kind of jump or sequence he wants to try. He may come up with something new.
- To play this game outside, find a playground that has a slide. Ask your child to go up the slide and come down (1) lifting his left hand in the air, (2) lifting left, then right hand in the air, (3) alternating left and right hands, then coming off the slide and hopping around to the stairs on his left foot, and so on until he's completed five instructions.
- In an open area, create an obstacle course using sticks and rocks. Have your child turn left or right around rocks or jump on his left or right foot over sticks. Let your child help set up the course.

Tips

- If your child struggles with the left-right concept, instruct him to march, saying "left, right, left, right" before jumping to hit a pillow.
- If your child is having trouble following instructions, let him jump on the bed while moving his left and right arms up and down and calling out "left, right."
- Use this game as a break from schoolwork or more challenging games. It may help your child blow off some steam or expend some pent-up energy.

WAR

It's war! On paper anyway. Despite its name, cooperation and consensus are the keys to a good battle.

Goals: Practice expressive language, sequencing, cause and effect, and reasoning; build fine motor skills; and strengthen memory.

Materials: Large paper; different-colored pencils, markers, crayons, or sidewalk chalk; a good imagination.

When/Where: Anytime, at home, at a playground, or anywhere you have a surface to write on and something to write with. The game works best with two players.

The Game: Setting up the page to play may take some time, but it's an important part of the game. This is a time of decision making and communication. Keep information flowing between players.

Place a large piece of paper, either horizontally or vertically, between you and your child. Together, decide where the battle will be fought (in the mountains, in the ocean, on another planet), then draw the battlefield. You don't need to be a good artist—a line can go a long way to suggest a mountain or stream. (See Figure 8.3.) Put in as much detail as you like, including castles and caves.

Next, players take turns selecting three fighters each for the battle and drawing them along the vertical margin of their side of the page. Fighters can be a favorite superhero, a doll, or an imaginary creature. As players draw, each must state who the fighter is and what special powers he has. Each character gets three powers. Players must pay attention to the characters their opponent picks so that they can create a strong team that will be able to attack and defend themselves in battle.

For example, player one may draw Ropeboy, whose hands shoot unbreakable rope that he can use to tie up an enemy. The rope can attach to any surface so he can swing. And he

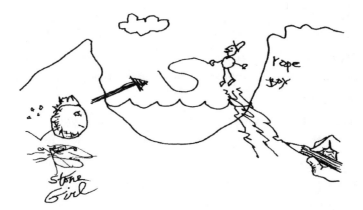

Figure 8.3 War

can jump really high. Player two then draws a character, explaining who she is and what powers she possesses: Stone-girl can turn into any type of stone or rock. She can roll in any direction and can break apart into pieces, which then come back together.

When each side has an army of three, you're ready to rumble! Player one selects a fighter and an opponent, describes an attack and a consequence of the attack. He must clearly articulate what the attacker will do and what the effect will be on his opponent: "Ropeboy will jump on top of the mountain. He will shoot his rope around Stonegirl and tie her up." Once the attack has been described, player one draws a line from Rope-boy to Stonegirl, then encircles her with lines to show that she has been tied.

Player two now has to make a countermove—for example, she can have Stonegirl turn to pebbles, which tumble out of the rope. Or she can choose a new fighter to attack Ropeboy or another member of her opponent's army, leaving Stonegirl to be saved on a later turn. Either way, she must describe the action and draw it.

Fighters can use only powers that were selected at the beginning of the game. So Ropeboy cannot suddenly make fire, and Stonegirl cannot turn into water if these were not initially assigned powers.

Once a character runs out of options, she is defeated (no one dies in this game). The victor draws an X over the conquered one. For example, if Ropeboy gets trapped in a net under a rock and his ropes have been burned up, he has run out of options.

The game is over when one player knocks out all of the other player's characters or when someone calls a truce. By the end of the game the page is usually a mess of lines, scratches, and squiggles.

Variations

- This game is wide open to variation. Create your own reality and ground rules.
- If you love history or mythology, suggest using characters like Joan of Arc or Hercules to enrich your child's knowledge of heroes from the past.
- Restrict one player to defensive moves while the other uses only attacks. See how creative you can be with your strategies under these conditions.
- After the war, write a story based on the events that took place.
- For longer battles, expand the number of fighters to five or more.
- For a faster-moving game, limit the number of times each character can use a particular power. Once the fighter has reached his limit, he must retire from the field.

Tips

- You can play in teams if there is more than one child in the house.
- If you wish, when you're first creating your characters, show by example how to create one that can counter an opponent's strengths. For example, if you know that Stonegirl can turn to pebbles, you might create Bubble Kid, who encases her enemies in giant unbreakable bubbles.

- For a child with fine-motor difficulty, this game is very freeing. She doesn't have to shape letters or write in a straight line on the page. The quality of the drawing is unimportant.
- Admitting defeat may be difficult for some children. Help your child see that there is a lot to be learned from missteps and mistakes.

AaBbCcDdEeFfGgHhIiJjKkLlMmNnOoPpQqRrSsTtUuVvWwXxYyZz

Appendix

The Alphabet

The basic things your child needs to know about the alphabet:

■ There are twenty-six letters, and each letter has a name.

■ The letters are arranged in a particular order that we call, naturally, *alphabetical order*.

■ When you see letters on a page, they can appear in different ways: in CAPITALS (or UPPERCASE) or in lowercase. Your child must be able to distinguish between them.

A   a   (apple)
B   b   (book)
C   c   (car)

D	d	(daddy)
E	e	(echo)
F	f	(finger)
G	g	(goat)
H	h	(hat)
I	i	(igloo)
J	j	(judge)
K	k	(kitty)
L	l	(licorice)
M	m	(mother)
N	n	(nose)
O	o	(ox)
P	p	(peacock)
Q	q	(queen) This letter is always followed by *u*
R	r	(rain)
S	s	(snake)
T	t	(toes)
U	u	(umbrella)
V	v	(violin)
W	w	(wind)
X	x	(x-ray)
Y	y	(yo-yo)
Z	z	(zebra)

Simple Basic Phonics: Vowels and Consonants

There are two types of letters in the alphabet: vowels and consonants. Reading teachers know a lot about the way they work, but for now, here are the most important things your child needs to learn about them:

There are five vowels: *a, e, i, o, u.*

When you say a vowel, you make the sound from inside your mouth without bringing your lips together. Try it: say "Oh! I see!" and pay attention to what your mouth does when you say "O" and "I" and "ee." Were your lips together or apart?

Children learn in school that there are long vowels (like the /ā/ in *apron*) and short vowels (like the /ă/ in *apple*). In dictionaries, the long vowel is written with a straight little line on top (*nāme*), and the short vowel is written with a little curved cap on top (*căt*), so you know which way to pronounce it.

But very often vowels make different sounds other than "long" and "short," depending on the other letters around them. Think about how the *a* sounds in *about* or when you say "Aaaah" at the doctor's office. Think about how the *o* sounds in *Ow!* or how the *o* sounds in *two*. Can you hear a difference?

But don't worry, your child will learn the many different sounds the vowels can make the more she practices with her teachers and special reading instructors and the more you read together at home.

The other twenty-one letters are consonants.

You make the sounds of the consonants in different ways. Sometimes you put your lips together and push air out of them (for example, when you say the /b/ in *bee* or the /p/ in *pop!*). Or sometimes you tap your tongue against your teeth (for example, when you say /t/ in *tea*). Or sometimes you do complicated things with your lips and your tongue and your teeth to make the sounds (for example, when you say *cloth, pluck,* or *blimp*).

Some consonants change their sound. *C* can make a hard sound, as in *cat, cup,* or *cotton,* or a soft sound, as in *cent* or *city.*

G also can make a hard sound, as in *game*, *got*, and *gum*, or a soft /j/ sound as in *gently*, *ginger*, and *gym*. Or sometimes it's not a matter of hard or soft—*s*, for example, can sound like a *hiss*, as in snake, or like a *zzz*, as in *as* or *is*.

And then there is *y*.

Sometimes *y* works like a vowel; sometimes it works like a consonant. It's a vowel in the word *my* because it sounds like a long /ī/. It's a vowel in the word *happy* because it sounds like a long /ē/. It's a consonant in the word *yes* because it sounds something like *yuh*.

Vowels for Vowel Games

Good readers can easily hear the sounds of the consonants when they read a word aloud—like the *c* and *t* in *cat* or the *b* and *g* in *bug*. To hear the sounds the vowels make is trickier, though.

For most children the long vowels are pretty easy to identify—for example, can you hear the long /ā/ in *day* or the long /ō/ in OK? It's as if the long vowel, when read or spoken, says its own name. However, short vowels are a different story— they make more subtle sounds that are harder for beginning and struggling readers and writers to recognize.

Think of the short /ă/ and the short /ĭ/ in *rabbit*. When you say *rabbit*, the short /ă/ is pronounced very quickly between the *r* and the *b*, the short /ĭ/ is squished between the *b* and the *t*. Most beginning readers, and struggling readers for sure, are more likely to hear the consonants—*r*, *b*, and *t*.

When you play games that focus on long and short vowels, make sure *you* are attuned to the sounds they make so that you can keep your child on the right track. If she has particular trouble with vowel sounds, exaggerate them as you play the game: for example, urge her to say r ă ă ă ă ă ă bbĭ ĭ ĭ ĭ ĭ t or c ā ā ā ā ā k.

Start with simple words with vowels that *you* can clearly identify as long or short. The short lists below can get you started. Even better, ask your child's teacher for a list of words she's working on in school. As your child progresses, you can up the ante by working with diphthongs and digraphs, discussed later in this Appendix.

Long ā Words

-*ace* words	face, lace, race, trace, space, place
-*ade* words	made, blade, grade, lemonade
-*age* words	rage, cage, page, stage
-*ake* words	cake, bake, make, take, rake, fake, snake
-*ale* words	tale, sale, whale, scale, exhale
-*ame* words	came, same, name, game, blame
-*ane* words	Jane, mane, lane, plane, insane
-*ape* words	cape, tape, shape, grape
-*ate* words	date, fate, mate, Kate, eliminate
-*ave* words	cave, gave, save, brave, shave (but not *have!*)
-*ai* words	rain, wait, raise, hair, mail, paint, maid (but not *said!*)
-*ay* words	say, day, pay, may, way

Short ă Words

-*ab* words	cab, tab, crab, grab
-*ad* words	bad, sad, mad, Dad, glad
-*ag* words	bag, hag, rag, snag

-*am* words	am, Sam, ham, yam, clam, swam
-*at* words	cat, fat, mat, sat, brat
-*ax* words	wax, Max, tax
-*ack* words	back, tack, crack, smack, attack
-*act* words	act, fact, pact, impact

Long ē Words

-*ee* words	bee, see, wee, free, tree, eel, peel, peek, wheel, deed, weed, seem, screech, queen, green, beep, deer, feet, sneeze, proceed
-*ea* words	eat, leaf, read, meat, pea, sea, flea, beak, sneak, beach, reach, real, steal, cream, team, teach, bean, mean, ear, clear, leap, please, feast, least (but be careful: the *e* in some -*ea* words is pronounced the short way, like He *read* the book yesterday; or in words like *head, bread, spread, bear*)
-*ief* words	thief, brief, chief, grief, relief

Y Words That Make the Long ē Sound

Some words that end in a consonant and a *y*—any, every, lady, body, funny, very, many, pretty, easy. And, of course . . .

The many -*ly* words—like only, really, usually, quickly, happily, especially

Short ĕ Words

-*ed* words	bed, fed, red, led, shed, Fred, sled
-*eg* words	beg, keg, peg, Meg
-*em* words	them, hem, stem, Clem
-*en* words	Ben, ten, den, men, then
-*eck* words	deck, peck, wreck, neck

-*ell* words	bell, tell, sell, well, yell, Jell-O
-*end* words	end, bend, mend, blend, send
-*ent* words	cent, went, tent, spent, accident
-*ess* words	dress, mess, bless, guess, fortress

Long ī Words

-*ie* words	pie, lie, tie, die
-*ice* words	ice, nice, mice, rice, slice, twice
-*ide* words	hide, ride, side, pride, slide, beside
-*ies* words	pies, flies, fries, tries, lies
-*ife* words	fife, life, rife, wife, knife
-*ike* words	bike, Mike, like, strike
-*igh* and -*ight* words	high, sigh, thigh, night, right, tight, flight
-*ile* words	pile, mile, smile, while
-*ime* words	dime, time, chime, slime
-*ine* words	mine, fine, pine, shine
-*ind* words	find, kind, mind, wind (like a clock—but not the *wind* that blows)
-*ipe* words	pipe, ripe, wipe, stripe
-*ire* words	fire, wire, hire, tire
-*ite* words	kite, bite, quite, white, impolite
-*ive* words	dive, five, hive, drive, alive (but not live as in "I *live* on Elm Lane.")

Y Words That Make the Long ī Sound

Some words that end in *y*—by, my, cry, fly, shy, spy, why, qualify, satisfy

| -*ye* words | bye, dye, eye, rye |

Short ĭ Words

-*ib* words	bib, crib, fib
-*id* words	did, kid, lid, slid
-*ig* words	big, pig, jig, wig, twig
-*im* words	him, Kim, swim, trim
-*in* words	pin, tin, chin, spin, clothespin
-*ip* words	lip, tip, trip, slip, unzip
-*it* words	it, bit, fit, quit, benefit
-*ix* words	mix, six, fix, Trix
-*ick* words	stick, trick, Dick, kick, pick, quick
-*ift* words	gift, lift, swift
-*ill* words	will, fill, pill, drill, skill, refill
-*imp* words	blimp, limp, chimp
-*ink* words	ink, pink, think, shrink
-*ish* words	fish, wish, dish, swish, foolish
-*iss* words	hiss, miss, kiss
-*ist* words	mist, list, twist, resist
-*itch* words	itch, witch, twitch

Long ō Words

-*o* words	go, no, so (but not *do*, *to*, or *who*)
-*oa* words	coach, road, toad, soak, coal, foam, Joan, roar, toast, goat
-*oke* words	joke, poke, broke, smoke, spoke
-*old* words	bold, fold, old, gold, hold, told
-*ole* words	mole, hole, pole, whole
-*oll* words	roll, toll, troll, stroll (but not *doll*)
-*olt* words	colt, jolt, molt
-*ome* words	home, gnome, Rome (but not *some*!)

-one words	bone, zone, phone, stone, postpone (but not *one*)
-ope words	hope, dope, nope, rope, slope, envelope
-ose or *-oze* words	nose, rose, froze, doze
-ost words	most, ghost, post (but not *frost* or *lost*)
-ove words	stove, wove, and drove (but not *love, dove,* or *shove*)
-ow words	bow, snow, slow, show, yellow (but not *cow, now,* or *how*)

Short ŏ Words

-ob words	Bob, job, knob, blob, slob
-od words	cod, nod, rod, plod
-og words	hog, log, frog, smog
-ot words	hot, got, not, spot, trot
-ox words	box, fox, ox, pox, phlox
-ock words	lock, rock, sock, block, flock, shock
-ond words	pond, fond, blond, frond, beyond (but not *second*)

Long ū Words

(Note: Long ū can sound like *you*, as in *use*, or like *oo*, as in *moo*.)

-ue words	cue, Sue, blue, glue, true, rescue
-ube words	cube, rube, tube
-ude words	rude, prude, Gertrude, attitude
-ule words	mule, rule, Yule
-une words	June, tune, prune

-use words	fuse, muse, use, refuse (but not *house*)
-ute words	cute, brute, chute, flute, dilute

Short ŭ Words

-ub words	cub, rub, tub, club, scrub
-ud words	cud, dud, mud, thud
-ug words	bug, dug, mug, rug, snug
-un words	bun, fun, run, sun, spun
-up words	cup, pup, sup
-us and *-uss* words	bus, plus, fuss, muss
-ut and *-utt* words	but or butt, cut, nut, hut, shut, mutt
-uck words	duck, luck, pluck, stuck, truck, yuck
-udge words	fudge, judge, smudge, trudge
-uff words	puff, fluff, gruff, stuff
-ull words	dull, gull, lull, mull (but not *bull*, *full*, or *pull*)
-um words	gum, hum, drum, plum, swum, chum
-umb words	dumb, numb, crumb, thumb
-ump words	jump, lump, pump, grump, slump, plump
-unch words	bunch, lunch, munch, crunch
-ung words	hung, rung, sung, stung, swung, flung
-unk words	bunk, hunk, junk, chunk, skunk
-unt words	hunt, runt, grunt, stunt
-ush words	hush, mush, brush, slush (but not *bush*)
-ust words	dust, must, rust, crust, trust

Consonant Blends

Beginning readers start with simple words such as *cat*, *sat*, *mop*—a single consonant next to a single vowel. As the words get more complicated, children will see two (or sometimes three) consonants in a row before seeing a vowel. In words such as **bl**ot, **st**ep, **ink**, **sl**ump, de**scr**ibe, the consonant *groups*—*bl*, *st*, *nk*, *sl*, *mp*, *scr*—are blended together when the word is read, which is why we call them *consonant blends*.

Blends may appear at the beginning, middle, or end of a word. In the following list are common consonant blends with examples that can help you add a more challenging element to basic phonics or spelling games.

Consonant Blends at the Beginning of Words

pr	as in	print, prank, pretty
tr	as in	trap, trip, tremble
gr	as in	grab, grateful, grin
br	as in	brat, brim, brag
cr	as in	crib, cry, crazy
dr	as in	drip, dress, draw
fr	as in	friend, fresh, frozen
st	as in	step, stump, stimulate
sp	as in	spit, spy, spirit
sk	as in	skin, skunk, skim
sc	as in	scatter, scant, scamper
sw	as in	swim, swallow, swell
sm	as in	smell, smitten, smack
sn	as in	snap, snare, snit
pl	as in	planet, plenty, plump
cl	as in	clap, clever, class
bl	as in	blab, blimp, blob

fl	as in	flip, fly, flatten
sl	as in	slam, slime, slip
gl	as in	glad, gloat, glimmer
str	as in	string, stranded, stress
scr	as in	screen, scribble, scram

Consonant Blends in the Middle of Words

bl	as in	oblige, emblem, ablaze
br	as in	library, umbrella, vibrate
cl	as in	include, eclipse, declare
cr	as in	secret, incredible, scarecrow
dr	as in	address, children, humdrum
fl	as in	aflame, inflate, snowflake
fr	as in	afraid, infrared, carefree
gl	as in	mangling, burglar, spyglass
gr	as in	degrade, hungry, fragrant
pl	as in	multiply, explain, complete
pr	as in	express, comprehend, April
sc	as in	escape, telescope, escalator
sl	as in	bobsled, asleep, snowslide
sp	as in	suspend, respect, inspire
st	as in	mistake, restful, instead
scr	as in	unscramble, describe, inscription

Consonant Blends at the End of Words

ld	as in	cold, build, meld
lf	as in	self, shelf, elf
sk	as in	ask, tusk, mask
st	as in	rest, fast, crust
nk	as in	sink, crank, plunk
nt	as in	rent, ant, grunt

mp as in ramp, dump, camp

ng as in sing, lung, rang

Digraphs, Diphthongs, and Silent Letters

Their names may sound formidable, but their meanings are simple. A digraph is two (and sometimes three) consonants or vowels that represent a single sound: for example, *th*—in *thing*, *ph*—in *phone*, *ee* in *weep*, *dge* in *fudge*.

A diphthong is two letters, almost always two vowels, that come together to make a different vowel sound: for example, *oy* in *toy*, *ow* in *cow*, and *ou* in *ought*.

You don't need to explain these terms to your child, but the more you play Wordplay games, the more you'll be able to identify digraphs and diphthongs. As you learn, be alert to the ones that give your child trouble. The following lists are examples of common digraph and diphthong patterns that are good to reinforce:

Digraphs

ay makes a long /ā/ sound, as in day, say, play

ai makes a long /ā/ sound, as in rain, Spain, plain

aw as in awful, lawn, law, straw

al makes an -*aw* sound, as in talk, walk, chalk, call, wall

au makes an -*aw* sound, as in August, automobile, cause, taught, dinosaur

oo as in look, took, wood, foot, cookie

oo as in food, school, tool, mood, boo, igloo

ou also makes an -*aw* sound in ought, bought, thought

ow makes the long /ō/ sound, as in show, blow, grow, tomorrow

ch as in children, pitcher, reach, cha-cha-cha

ph sounds like /f/ in phone, photo, alphabet, autograph, telegraph

sh as in she, ship, wish, crash

th as in the, that, this, mother, father, weather, smooth

wh as in what, where, why, whisper, cartwheel

Diphthongs

ow as in cow, now, towel, shower, eyebrow

ou also makes an *ow* sound as in out, our, ouch, count, cloud, house, mouse, louse

oy as in boy, toy, joy, soy

oi as in oil, point, boil, spoil

Silent letters, of course, don't make any sound at all: the *gh* in *light, eight, high, thought*; the *k* in *knife, know, knickers*; the *w* in *write, wrist, wrong*; and the final *e* in a whole lot of words, such as *bake, bike, people, because, write, home*.

Sight Words

Sight words are words that usually cannot be sounded out; they must be memorized. The following one hundred words are the most commonly used sight words in English. They are listed in order, starting with the most frequently used in writing. There are many more sight words that your child will need to know as she becomes a more proficient reader.

the	a	you
of	to	that
and	is	he

was	how	my
for	their	than
are	will	first
as	other	water
with	about	been
his	out	call
they	many	who
I	then	oil
be	them	its
this	these	now
have	so	find
from	some	long
or	her	down
one	would	day
by	make	get
word	like	come
but	into	made
what	time	may
all	has	part
were	look	over
we	two	new
when	more	sound
your	write	take
said	go	only
there	see	little
use	number	work
each	no	know
which	way	place
she	could	year
do	people	live

Confusable Words and Letters

Struggling readers often confuse sight words (see "Sight Words" in this Appendix) that have similar visual patterns, such as *that* and *what*, *for* and *from*. They may also confuse the letters *b*, *d*, and *p* and read words beginning or ending with these letters incorrectly.

The words below are grouped with those that commonly cause confusion for young readers. Many more word groups will confound a particular child. You should keep a list of the words your child confuses for use in Wordplay games.

went, want, was	where, when
the, they, then, there	who, what
our, are	a, the
no, not	a, and
him, his	do, don't
her, here	in, on
here, there	go, got, gone
then, when	you, your
when, what	old, odd
what, that	have, has, had
was, saw	do, don't, does
one, on	says, said
one, once	come, can
of, for	big, dig, pig
for, from	bug, dug, pug
of, off	dad, bad, pad, dab
was, is	sad, sap
was, were, where	dip, did, bid
do, does	dog, bog

Word Families

Like aunts, uncles, and cousins, words in families are related to each other—through their spelling patterns. For example, simple -at words are in one family (bat, rat, sat); -it words in another (hit, knit, sit).

Nursery rhymes and many books for young children draw on common word families to teach patterns of spelling and reading. (For example, the great Dr. Seuss drew on that -at family when he wrote The Cat in the Hat.)

The following list of common word families is for any game that focuses on phonics, rhyming, and spelling. Pay attention to the exceptions, though. There are always a few black sheep in word families to be avoided (think of car, far—and war). Other word families can be pronounced more than one way (think of lead and read—with a long /ē/ sound (as in "you can lead a horse to water. . . .")—and dead, lead, and read, with a short /ĕ/ sound, as in "I read the book yesterday").

A Families

-ack: attack, back, black, crack, Jack, knack, lack, pack, quack, rack, sack, snack, stack, tack, track, whack, Zack

-ad: ad, bad, Chad, dad, glad, had, lad, mad, pad, sad, tad

-am: am, bam, dam, ham, jam, ram, Sam, slam, wham, Pam

-an: an, ban, Fran, clan, fan, Dan, ran, tan, man, Stan

-ap: cap, clap, flap, gap, lap, map, nap, rap, sap, tap

-at: at, bat, brat, cat, chat, fat, flat, hat, mat, pat, rat, sat, Sprat, tat, that, vat

-*ank*: bank, blank, crank, Hank, plank, prank, rank, sank, spank, tank, thank

-*ash*: ash, bash, cash, dash, gash, hash, lash, mash, rash, sash

-*ail*: fail, hail, Gail, jail, mail, nail, pail, rail, sail, snail, tail, wail

-*ale*: bale, dale, Gale, male, pale, sale, stale, tale

-*ain*: brain, gain, main, pain, plain, rain, Spain, train

-*ake*: bake, brake, cake, flake, Jake, lake, make, rake, shake, stake, take, wake

-*ame*: came, blame, fame, game, lame, Mame, name, same, shame, tame

-*ate*: ate, crate, date, fate, grate, hate, Kate, late, mate, Nate, plate, skate, state

-*ay*: bay, bray, clay, day, gray, hay, lay, May, pay, play, ray, say, spray, stay, sway, tray, way

-*aw*: claw, flaw, gnaw, jaw, law, paw, raw, saw, slaw, straw

-*all*: ball, call, fall, hall, mall, stall, tall, wall

-*ar*: bar, car, far, jar, mar, par, star, tar (but not *war*!)

E Families

-*ell*: bell, cell, dell, dwell, fell, pell-mell, sell, smell, spell, swell, tell, well

-*en*: Ben, den, fen, Gwen, hen, Ken, men, pen, ten, wren, Zen

-*ent*: bent, cent, dent, gent, Kent, lent, pent, rent, sent, tent, vent, went

-*est*: best, fest, jest, nest, pest, quest, rest, test, vest, west, zest

-*er*: per, her, permanent, ever, mother, over, water, offer

-*eat*: beat, cleat, eat, feat, heat, meat, neat, peat, seat,
  wheat (but not *great!*)
-*eep*: beep, deep, jeep, keep, peep, sheep, sleep, steep,
  weep
-*eel*: feel, heel, keel, kneel, peel, reel, wheel

I *Families*

-*ick*: kick, lick, nick, pick, quick, Rick, sick, slick, stick,
  tick, thick, trick, wick
-*ip*: blip, clip, dip, grip, hip, lip, nip, pip, quip, rip, sip,
  ship, slip, Skip, tip, trip, whip, zip
-*it*: bit, fit, flit, hit, kit, knit, lit, nit, pit, quit, sit, spit,
  slit, snit, writ, zit
-*im*: brim, him, Jim, Kim, rim, swim, trim, vim, whim
-*in*: bin, din, grin, in, gin, kin, Min, pin, shin, spin,
  thin, tin, win
-*ill*: Bill, fill, hill, ill, Jill, kill, mill, pill, quill, sill, still,
  till, will
-*ice*: dice, lice, mice, nice, price, rice, slice, thrice, twice,
  vice
-*ide*: bride, hide, pride, ride, side, slide, tide, wide
-*ight*: bright, delight, fight, flight, fright, light, might,
  night, right, sight, slight, tight, tonight
-*ile*: file, mile, Nile, pile, rile, smile, stile, tile, vile, while
-*ine*: dine, fine, line, mine, nine, pine, swine, tine, vine
-*ing*: bring, cling, fling, king, ping, ring, sing, sling,
  spring, sting, string, swing, thing, wing, zing
-*ink*: blink, brink, ink, link, mink, pink, rink, sink,
  think, wink
-*ir*: fir, skirt, Virginia, dirty, whir, circle, girl

O *Families*

-op: bop, cop, crop, clop, drop, flop, hop, lop, mop, Pop, sop, stop, top

-og: bog, cog, clog, fog, frog, grog, hog, jog, log, slog (but not *dog*)

-ot: blot, cot, dot, got, hot, jot, lot, not, pot, plot, rot, shot, spot, tot

-ock: block, clock, cock, dock, flock, frock, hock, jock, lock, mock, pock, rock, sock, stock, shock, tock

-oke: awoke, bloke, broke, Coke, joke, poke, spoke, stoke, stroke, woke

-oat: boat, coat, float, goat, gloat, moat, oat, throat

-oo: boo, coo, goo, loo, moo, shoo, too, zoo

-ook: book, brook, cook, crook, hook, look, nook, rook, shook, took

-oom: boom, bloom, broom, doom, gloom, loom, room, zoom

-oop: coop, droop, goop, hoop, loop, oops, poop, scoop, snoop, stoop, troop, whoop, nincompoop

-ore: bore, core, chore, fore, lore, more, ore, pore, sore, shore, store, tore, wore

-out: about, bout, gout, lout, out, pout, rout, shout, spout, stout, tout

-ow (as in *cow*): bow, cow, how, now, sow, vow, wow, plow, chow

-oil: boil, broil, coil, foil, oil, soil, spoil, toil

-ow (as in *crow*): blow, crow, flow, glow, grow, low, mow, row, show, slow, snow, sow, stow, throw, tow

-own: brown, crown, down, drown, frown, gown, nightgown, town

-*or*: for, short, or, order, north, important, horn,
   Oregon, orbit

U *Families*

-*uck*: buck, duck, luck, muck, puck, pluck, suck, stuck,
   tuck, truck, yuck

-*ug*: bug, dug, glug, hug, jug, lug, mug, pug, rug, snug,
   tug

-*um*: bum, chum, gum, hum, mum, rum, sum, tummy-
   tum-tum, yum

-*ump*: bump, clump, dump, frump, hump, jump, lump,
   mumps, pump, rump, stump, trump

-*unk*: bunk, clunk, dunk, flunk, gunk, junk, lunk, punk,
   plunk, sunk, skunk, slunk, shrunk, trunk

-*ur*: blur, fur, sturdy, surf, purpose, nurse, Thursday,
   purple, turkey, curb

And some more

-*ould*: would, could, should

-*ought*: ought, bought, thought, fought, sought, brought

-*ield*: yield, shield, field

-*ough*: rough, enough, tough

-*eigh*: weigh, sleigh, inveigh

Prefixes, Suffixes, and Roots

Prefixes and suffixes are little add-ons to the main part, or root,
of words, that change or qualify the root's meaning. We add
prefixes to the beginning of root words and suffixes to the end.
Learning the meaning of simple prefixes and suffixes helps a

struggling reader expand his vocabulary and understand the building blocks of words.

To help your child become familiar with very basic prefixes, suffixes, and roots, start with simple concepts like the prefix *re-* (to "repeat" something) in front of a whole bunch of root verbs (*rewrite, redo, retell, rethink, reheat*). How does adding *re-* change the meaning of the root words *write, do, tell, think,* and *heat?* Then show how the suffix *-s* makes a plural out of almost any noun (remember, though, that some nouns require an *-es*, like *foxes*, or change form, like *mouse/mice*).

Handy Prefixes

contra- means "against" in words like *contradict, contraband, contrary*

dis- means "not" in words like *dishonest, dislike, disapprove, disagree*

fore- means "before" in words like *foresight, foreknowledge, foretell*

mid- means "in the middle of" in words like *midnight, midway, midsummer*

mis- suggests that something is "wrong" or "bad" in words like *misunderstand, mispronounce, mislead, misjudge*

pre- means "before" in words like *preview, prepare, predict, preheat*

re- means "to do again" in words like *retell, rewind, rework, rewrite*

un- means "not" in words like *unhappy, unwell, unlucky, unfriendly, unsure*

inter- means "between" in words like *international, intervene, interact, intercede sub-* means "under" in words like *submit, submarine, substandard*

super- means "above" or "greater than" in words like *supernatural, Superman, superhuman*

trans- means "across" in words like *transport, transcontinental, translate*

ultra- means "beyond" in words like *ultrasonic, ultrashort, ultrared*

anti- means "against" in words like *antidote, antitoxin, antifreeze, antisocial*

hyper- means "over or beyond" in words like *hyperactive, hyperbole, hypersensitive*

multi- means "many" in words like *multiply, multiple, multiskilled*

omni- means "all" in words like *omnivore, omnipotent, omniscient*

Handy Suffixes

-s means "plural" or "more than one of something" in nouns like *brothers* and *sisters, books, toys, apples* (although some nouns add an *-es* to make a plural, such as *foxes, wishes, watches*) Note: don't let your child confuse the plural *-s* with the *-s* you add to verb forms, such as *he walks.*

-ed shows that something happened in the past in verbs like *walked, talked, danced, worked*

-able means "capable of being or tending to be" in adjectives like *durable, drinkable, comfortable, lovable*

-arium means "a place for keeping something" in nouns like *aquarium, terrarium, planetarium, dolphinarium*

-tion means "the state or condition of something" in nouns like *completion* (the state of being finished), *information* (what you get when you're being informed), *inspiration* (the state of being inspired), *exhaustion* (the state of being really, really tired)

-dom also means "the state or condition of something" in nouns like *freedom* (being free), *boredom* (being bored), *wisdom* (being wise)

-er and *-or* mean a "doer" in nouns like *teacher* (the one who does the teaching), *dancer* (the one who does the dancing), *actor* (the one who does the acting), and *player* (the one who plays)

-ful means "full of" in adjectives like *wonderful, gleeful, thoughtful, hateful, wishful*

-hood means "being in a state or condition of" in nouns like *motherhood, brotherhood, neighborhood*

-ing means "doing something" in verbs or verblike nouns such as *dancing, painting, reading, thinking*

-ity means "the state or condition of" in nouns like *purity, authority, monstrosity, humidity*

-ish means "somewhat" in adjectives like *foolish, ticklish, selfish, squeamish*

-graphy means "writing or recording" in adjectives like *calligraphy, photography, geography*

-less means "without" in adjectives like *nameless, joyless, headless, heartless, clueless*

-logy means "the study of" in nouns like *biology, geology, psychology*

-ly means "having the quality or characteristics of" in adjectives like *beastly, queenly, cowardly, writerly*

-*ness* means "being in a state or condition of something" in nouns like *happiness, darkness, gentleness, thoughtfulness*

-*scope* means "seeing or viewing" in nouns like *telescope, microscope, radarscope*

-*some* means "full of" in adjectives like *quarrelsome, loathsome, troublesome, meddlesome*

-*vore* means "an eater of" in nouns like *carnivore, herbivore, omnivore* (you can also see it used as a prefix in words like *voracious*, meaning "greedy in eating")

-*ward* points to a certain direction, as in *backward, forward, downward, westward*

Simple Roots

Come—Prefixes: *become, overcome, income, outcome*
Suffixes: *coming* (note that the final *e* disappears), *comes*

Connect—Prefixes: *reconnect, disconnect, interconnect*
Suffixes: *connecting, connection, connector*

Do—Prefixes: *undo, redo, overdo.* Suffixes: *doable, doing, doer*

Cook—Prefixes: *overcook, undercook, precook.* Suffixes: *cooker, cooked, cooking*

Joy—Prefixes: *enjoy, overjoyed.* Suffixes: *joyful, joyless, joyfulness*

Play—Prefixes: *replay, downplay, interplay.* Suffixes: *player, played, playing, playful, playfulness*

Read—Prefixes: *reread, misread.* Suffixes: *reader, reading, readable, readability*

Sight—Prefixes: *foresight, insight, hindsight.* Suffixes: *sighted, sightless, sights*

Step—Prefixes: *overstep, misstep, instep*. Suffixes: *stepping, stepper, steps*

Take—Prefixes: *retake, mistake, undertake*. Suffixes: *taking* (note the final *e* disappears), *taker*

Use—Prefixes: *misuse, reuse, overuse*. Suffixes: *useful, useless, used, user*

View—Prefixes: *preview, interview, overview, review*. Suffixes: *viewed, views, viewing, viewer*

Word—Prefixes: *reword, foreword*. Suffixes: *wording, words, wordy, wordless*

Write—Prefixes: *rewrite, miswrite, underwrite, overwrite*. Suffixes: *writer, writing, writerly*

Parts of Speech

Understanding the way our language is organized into different parts of speech helps children comprehend stories and write clear sentences and paragraphs. Try to point out the different types of words as you and your child read together and as you play some of the Wordplay games.

Here is a simple refresher course for those of you who haven't thought about grammar since *you* were in school.

Nouns can be a person, place, or thing—and then some! Nouns can also be states of mind, activities, feelings, thoughts, ideas, systems, institutions—such as *love, tae-kwon-do, hunger, inspiration, belief, health care, bureaucracy*. Nouns can be common—that is, they refer to something in general (*aunt, city, game, religion*)—or proper, referring to someone or something in particular (*Aunt Claire, San Francisco, Monopoly, Buddhism*). Proper nouns always begin with a capital letter.

Pronouns stand in for nouns—*I, you, he, she, it, we, they* can be subjects of sentences (***We** are delighted to be here*); *me, you, him, her, it, us,* and *them* are objective pronouns and often come after prepositions like *to, after, between,* and so on (*We were delighted to see **them**; This is between you and **me***). Other pronouns are *several, someone, who, whom, which, what,* and *whose*—because all these words can fill in for nouns. Think of *Several are rotten* (*several* standing in for apples).

Verbs are commonly defined as "action words"; they can also describe a state of being or a feeling. For example, in the sentence ***She dances*** or *She **is dancing***, most children will grasp that dance is the action and therefore the verb. But in sentences like *Who's there?* the verb (*to be*—who *is*, which describes a state of being) may be harder to find.

Adjectives enrich nouns by describing them in some way. A pie doesn't sound like much, but add adjectives: *fragrant, juicy, golden, apple*—and suddenly that pie is much more appealing, as long as you like apples, that is. Adjectives give us more information about the noun—its appearance (*gray* parrot), its quantity (*six* parrots), and other details (*six noisy, hungry gray* parrots).

Adverbs work mostly with adjectives and verbs similar to the way adjectives work with nouns: they make them even more vivid. *Ill* isn't a pleasant adjective to begin with and "She was *ill*" is bad enough, but "She was *extremely ill*" sounds so much more serious. "She was eating" sounds uninteresting, but if we know "she was eating *voraciously*," we get the idea she was *very, very* hungry. Some common adverbs are *very, more, often, never, too,* and words ending in *-ly,* such as *happily* and *beautifully.*

Articles are those tiny words—*a, an, the*—that pop up before common nouns and that struggling readers often stumble over. Grammarians call *a* and *an* **indefinite** articles. "Bring me *a* skateboard" or "Pick *an* apple" could call for any old skateboard or any old apple, which is why *a*—or *an*—is indefinite. *The* is **definite** because when you say "Bring me *the* skateboard," you're thinking of a specific one.

A and *an* mean the same thing, but we add the *n* when the word that follows the article begins with a vowel: an *a*pple, an *e*gret, an *i*cicle, an *o*pen door, an *u*nopened umbrella.

Conjunction: A junction is a place where things come together. A conjunction or connecting word brings words or phrases together. *And, or, but, because, after, however*—all are common conjunctions. Peanut butter *and* jelly wouldn't be a team without one.

Prepositions: These are small but important words—including *to, of, at, against, before*, etc.—that pop up before nouns or pronouns. They can indicate a position, a direction, a time lapse—and many other things. For example, the preposition *to* indicates *to whom* I gave something (I gave the book *to* a friend) or where I am going (*to* my friend's birthday party). Other prepositions, such as *over, above, toward, beyond*, show direction: The blue jay flew *over* my head *toward* the tree. Some indicate time or sequence: I went to the movie *after* lunch.

Interjection: Heavens to Betsy! Interjections are words that we just come out with to issue an order, or to express a feeling or a reaction to something. *Wow! Look! Gee whiz!* are good examples. (You can find lots more in action comic books!) And, hey! Interjections are always followed by an exclamation point!

A word of warning about parts of speech: There are times when the same word may function differently depending on how it is used. Your child may notice, for example, that *apple* is used as a noun in the sentence *This apple is yummy* but as an adjective (describing word) in the sentence *I want some more apple pie.*

The Basic Sentence

Sentences take many forms and can be made up of a single word—*Stop!*—or several dozen words. But when you play sentence games or writing games with your child, don't complicate things. Just keep your eye on the basics.

The rule of thumb is that a sentence must have a subject (a noun or pronoun) and a verb: (**She** *swims* well. **He** *reads* lots of books. **Mom** *loves* chocolate.)

The subject is the someone or something the sentence is about. The verb tells what that someone or something is thinking, feeling, doing, or just being. (Gracie *sang* to herself. The train *was speeding* along the tracks. I *am* in the third grade.)

Sentences can take several different forms. There are three common types of sentence that can be easily reinforced through games:

- **Declarative** sentences state something: *The snow is six inches deep. There's a bug in my soup.* These sentences end in a period.
- **Interrogative** sentences ask a question: *Are we there yet? Can I watch a video?* These end in a question mark.

■ **Imperative** sentences request or demand something:
Stop tickling your brother! Please eat your broccoli. Listen!
These end with an exclamation point or a period,
depending on the intensity of the demand or request.

Recommended Reading

n this book we've provided basic information about the many different aspects of reading that your child will need to master. If you have the time and the interest, there's a lot more you can learn about reading and learning differences. The following list cites the books we found most helpful. We've also included a sampling of children's books that may help your child learn the alphabet more easily, discover new words, and practice phonics.

As of this writing, everything we recommend is in print and available in book stores and online. However, if you discover that a book has been discontinued, check used book stores in your area or on the Web. We also encourage you and your child to find many, many other books at your local library or bookstore.

Alphabet Books

Don't limit your child to just one. Different authors present the alphabet in different ways. Find the ones that appeal most to your young reader. These are some of our favorites.

Base, Graeme. *Animalia.* Abrams Books for Young Readers, 1987.

Hubbard, Woodleigh. *C is for Curious: An ABC of Feelings.* Chronicle Books, 1990.

Martin, Bill, Jr., and John Archambault. *Chicka Chicka Boom Boom.* Simon & Schuster, 1989. (May be available in different editions.)

Seuss, Dr. *Dr. Seuss's ABC.* Beginner Books, Random House, 1996.

Thornhill, Jan. *The Wildlife ABC: A Nature Alphabet Book.* Half Moon Books, 1994.

Van Allsburg, Chris. *The Z Was Zapped: A Play in Twenty-Six Acts.* Houghton Mifflin, 1994.

Fun Books for Phonics

Some books for beginning readers target phonics, word families, and rhyming in inventive ways. Included should be anything by Dr. Seuss in the Beginner Books series (Random House). Also be aware that Scholastic provides a selection of discounted books to many schools. Included in these offerings are several entertaining phonics books, which are not always available at local bookstores. Check your child's school backpack for the Scholastic Books order forms. Here are just a few others:

Busch, Laura Callahan. Ready for Reading! series. Back
   Pack Books—Michael Friedman Publishing.
Serfozo, Mary. *The Big Bug Dug*. Scholastic, Inc., 2001.
Shaw, Nancy. Sheep series. Houghton Mifflin Company.
   Sheep Out to Eat, *Sheep in a Jeep*, and *Sheep Take a Hike*
   are some of the titles in this series.
Stamper, Judith Bauer. *Space Race*. Scholastic, Inc., 1998.

Books That Stretch Children's Vocabulary

Our favorite books to read with children are the ones by
authors who use language creatively and include tantalizing
words. Anything by William Steig in addition to the two listed
here, any unabridged edition of Rudyard Kipling's *Just So Stories*, and any unabridged edition of Oscar Wilde's children's stories are high on our list, along with the following:

Hergé. The Adventures of Tintin series. Little, Brown and
   Company.
Segal, Lore, editor. *The Juniper Tree and Other Tales from
   Grimm*. Farrar, Straus and Giroux, 1976.
Steig, William. *Rotten Island*. David R. Godine, 1984.
Steig, William. *The Zabajaba Jungle*. Farrar, Straus and
   Giroux, 1987.

Children's Reference Books

Many Wordplay games call for the use of reference books—a
habit you definitely want your child to acquire. These are the
most recent editions of the ones we like best.

The American Heritage Children's Dictionary. Houghton Mifflin Company, 1998.

Beal, George. *Kingfisher First Dictionary.* Larousse Kingfisher Chambers, 2001.

Bollard, John K. *Scholastic Student Thesaurus.* Scholastic, 2002.

Crawley, Angela, ed. *Kingfisher First Thesaurus.* Larousse Kingfisher Chambers, 1998.

DK Children's Illustrated Encyclopedia. Dorling Kindersley, 1998.

DK Merriam-Webster Children's Dictionary. Dorling Kindersley, 2000.

Hoare, Ben, ed. *The Kingfisher A-Z Encyclopedia.* Larousse Kingfisher Chambers, 2002.

Latimer, Jonathan P., and Karen Stray Nolting, eds. *Simon and Schuster Thesaurus for Children.* Simon and Schuster, 2001.

National Geographic United States Atlas for Young Explorers. National Geographic, 1999.

The Reader's Digest Children's Atlas of the World. Reader's Digest, updated version.

Time for Kids Magazine, ed. *Time for Kids World Almanac 2003: with Information Please.* Time Inc. Home Entertainment, 2003.

Wittels, Harriet, and Joan Greisman. *A First Thesaurus.* Golden Books, 1985.

Books That Complement Some of the Wordplay Games

Ahlberg, Janet, and Allan Ahlberg. *The Jolly Postman: Or Other People's Letters.* Little, Brown, 1986. This book has

"real" letters written in a variety of formats—a great
partner to the game Writing, Writing Everywhere.

Mosel, Arlene, as retold by. *Tikki Tikki Tembo*. Henry Hold
& Co., 1988. A fun story about memory.

Moss, Marissa. *My Notebook with Help From Amelia*. Pleasant
Company Publications, 1999. Designed to be written in
by your child with notes and tips from Amelia.

In the Toy Store

Look for products by the company *Creativity for Kids*, which
makes craft kits for children to create their own books and
diaries.

In addition to standard games that work directly on building word skills such as Boggle and Scrabble Jr., don't forget
games that work on the more discrete skills of memory (any
Concentration-type game), association (Outburst Jr.—a fast-
paced categories game), coordination (Twister—a great left-
right workout for hands and feet), and fine motor skills (Jenga
or Pick-Up Sticks).

Books on the Mechanics of Reading and Writing

These books are for adults who want to learn more about phonics, grammar, and the writing process. Included in several of
the books are activities for teachers to use with their students.
You should gauge the "fun factor" for yourself before asking
your child to try the activities.

Fry, Edward Bernard, Ph.D.; Jacqueline E. Kress, Ed.D., and
Dona Lee Fountoukidis, Ed.D. *Reading Teacher's Book of
Lists*, (4th Edition). Jossey-Bass, 2000.

Gordon, Karen Elizabeth. *The Deluxe Transitive Vampire: The
Ultimate Handbook of Grammar for the Innocent, the Eager,
and the Doomed.* Pantheon Books, 1993.

Gordon, Karen Elizabeth. *The New Well-Tempered Sentence:
A Punctuation Handbook for the Innocent, the Eager, and the
Doomed.* Ticknor and Fields, 1993.

Muschla, Gary Robert. *The Writing Teacher's Book of Lists:
With Ready-to-Use Activities and Worksheets.* Jossey-Bass,
1991.

Stull, Elizabeth Crosby. *Let's Read! A Complete Month by
Month Activities Program for Beginning Readers.* Center for
Applied Research in Education, 2000.

Sunflower, Cherlyn. *Really Writing! Ready to Use Writing
Process Activities for the Elementary Grades.* Center for
Applied Research in Education, 1994.

Books on Thinking and Learning Differently

If you want more information about the complexities of thinking and learning, these books are invaluable resources—and
encouraging:

Hall, Susan L., and Louisa C. Moats, Ed.C. *Parenting a Struggling Reader: A Guide to Diagnosis and Finding Help for Your
Child's Reading Difficulties.* Broadway Books, 2002.

Levine, Mel. *A Mind at a Time.* Simon and Schuster, 2002.

Smith, Corinne, Ph.D., and Lisa Strick. *Learning Disabilities,
A to Z: A Parent's Guide to Learning Disabilities from
Preschool to Adulthood.* Simon and Schuster, 1999.
West, Thomas G. *In the Mind's Eye: Visual Thinkers, Gifted
People with Dyslexia and Other Learning Difficulties,
Computer Images and the Ironies of Creativity.* Prometheus
Books, 1997.

Websites

If you type the keywords *children with learning disabilities* in the
search box on any search engine page, you'll turn up hundreds,
if not thousands, of sites to explore. For now, start with these:

aacap.org—website for the American Academy of
Child and Adolescent Psychiatry.

allkindsofminds.org—All Kinds of Minds is an insti-
tute for the understanding of differences in learning.

familyeducation.com—website that has an LD
weekly E-mail newsletter and a special page on
learning disabilities.

interdys.org—website for the International Dyslexia
Association. Interdys.org/disonly.stm is a site for kids
only.

AaBbCcDdEeFfGgHhIiJjKkLlMmNnOoPpQqRrSsTtUuVvWwXxYyZz

Index